THE DA VINCI CODE: FACT OR FICTION?

You've seen the movie.
You've read the book.
Now discover the truth!

THE DA VINCI CODE

FACT OR FICTION?

Hank Hanegraaff
& Paul L. Maier

TYNDALE HOUSE PUBLISHERS, INC., CAROL STREAM, ILLINOIS

Visit Tyndale's exciting Web site at www.tyndale.com

TYNDALE and Tyndale's quill logo are registered trademarks of Tyndale House Publishers, Inc.

The Da Vinci Code: Fact or Fiction?

The content on pages 42–50 and 59–65 is partially adapted from Hank Hanegraaff, *Resurrection* (Nashville: W Publishing Group, 2000).

The content on pages 51–56 is partially adapted from Hank Hanegraaff, *The Bible Answer Book* (Nashville: J. Countryman, 2004).

The content on pages 57–59 is partially adapted from Hank Hanegraaff, "Answering More Prime Time Fallacies," *Christian Research Journal*, Vol. 23/No. 2.

The content on pages 66–68 is partially adapted from Hank Hanegraaff, *The FACE that Demonstrates the Farce of Evolution* (Nashville: Word Publishing, 1998).

The content on pages 69–71 is partially adapted from Hank Hanegraaff, *The Bible Answer Book* (Nashville: J. Countryman, 2004).

Edited by Jeremy Taylor

Designed by RULE 29 with Dean H. Renninger

ISBN-13: 978-1-4143-0279-9 ISBN-10: 1-4143-0279-7

Printed in the United States of America

10 09 08 07 06
12 11 10 9 8

CONTENTS

FOREWORD

by Hank Hanegraaff

WHEN MEL GIBSON produced *The Passion of the Christ*—a movie that substantially follows the contours of the New Testament accounts of Jesus' death—he became the immediate subject of controversy. Leon Wieseltier, the literary editor of *The New Republic*, called *The Passion* "a repulsive, masochistic fantasy, a sacred snuff film" that is "without any doubt an anti-Semitic movie."[1] Maureen Dowd, writing in *The New York Times*, accused Gibson of "courting bigotry in the name of sanctity."[2] And Andy Rooney of *60 Minutes* fame characterized Gibson as "a real nut case" whose ulterior motive was making money.[3]

Conversely, when Dan Brown released *The Da Vinci Code*[4]—a novel that characterizes the New Testament Gospels as "fabrications" and the deity of Christ as a fable—he was immediately lauded as a brilliant historian. *Library Journal* characterized his work as "a compelling blend of history and page-turning suspense," a "masterpiece" that "should be mandatory reading."[5] *Publisher's Weekly* called it "an exhaustively researched page-turner about secret religious societies, ancient cover-ups and savage vengeance."[6] And best-selling author Nelson DeMille christened *The Da Vinci Code* "pure genius."[7]

Why is *The Passion* excoriated and *The Da Vinci Code* extolled? Why are Gibson's motives denounced and Brown's dignified? Why is Christ's passion referred to as a "repulsive, masochistic fantasy" and his supposed marriage to Mary Magdalene touted as a researched material fact? The answer may surprise you. It is not just that in our increasingly secularist culture it has become politically correct to cast aspersions on Christ and the church he founded. It is because of a great reversal of values. Fiction—such as the notion that Christianity was concocted to subjugate women—is being cleverly peddled as fact, while fact—such as the deity of Christ—is being capriciously passed off as fiction.

Nearly all of Brown's assertions in *The Da Vinci Code* are based on several statements he presents on page 1 under the heading of "FACT"—before the novel even begins. Most notable among these "facts" is the following:

> The Priory of Sion—a European secret society founded in 1099—is a real organization. In 1975 Paris's Bibliothèque Nationale discovered parchments known as *Les Dossiers Secrets*, identifying numerous members of the Priory of Sion, including Sir Isaac Newton, Botticelli, Victor Hugo, and Leonardo da Vinci.

At first blush, this may seem rather harmless. But Brown uses this "fact" (which in reality is completely untrue) to cast aspersions on Jesus Christ, the historicity of the Gospels, and the uniqueness of Christianity. Brown depicts the Priory of Sion as a secret society bent on covering up the scandal of Christ's marriage to Mary Magdalene—who would have been the true leader of the church if she had not unceremoniously crashed into an apostolic glass ceiling erected by a patriarchal church. As we will see, much of what Brown trumpets as truth is based on a fabrication concocted by an anti-Semite with a criminal record. Yet Brown says he is so confident in the reliability of his claims that were he to write a nonfiction piece on the same theme, he would not change a thing.[8]

The fact that *The Da Vinci Code* is false does not, of course, prove that Christianity is true. Thus, this book is divided into two sections. The first is a fast-paced analysis of Brown's "facts." To thoroughly examine the question of the historical authenticity of the claims made in *The Da Vinci Code*, I called on an expert witness—my good friend Dr. Paul Maier. As a highly regarded professor of ancient history and an award-winning author, Dr. Maier is in a unique position to unmask the deceptions of *The Da Vinci Code*. His rapier-sharp wit and his colorful style not only make Part 1 an engaging read but also highlight the disdain we both share for historical revisionism. The second section is an apologetic for what we know to be the *truth*. Here I provide a positive defense of the faith—namely, that the Bible is divine rather than human in origin, that Jesus Christ is God in human flesh, and that amid the religions of the ancient world, Christianity is demonstrably unique. Let me be clear: *no one should feel that his faith has been undermined by the fantasies and lies presented under the guise of truth in this novel.*

Finally, a word about my passion for this project. During one of my early morning treks to Starbucks, a young woman pulled me aside and, fighting tears, asked me to reassure her that the Christian faith was valid. She, along with a group of her friends, had read *The Da Vinci Code* and was seriously shaken by its assertions. That same morning Ron Beers, Senior Vice President at Tyndale House Publishers, called to tell me about an avalanche of inquiries his office had received regarding *The Da Vinci Code*—and to urge me to provide a response. Further solidifying my resolve to debunk this novel and defend the faith was my final conversation with my friend Bob Passantino. In his view this project was necessary not only because *The Da Vinci Code* is a runaway bestseller (as of this writing the book has sold more than 6 million copies, and film director Ron Howard is working in collaboration with Columbia Pictures to turn it into a major movie) but because the novel is on the vanguard of a growing movement seeking to reconstruct Christ, reinvent Christianity, and reject the canon of Scripture.

Bob not only encouraged me to write a response to Brown's book but also exhorted me to redouble my efforts to defend the faith. One hour later, a massive heart attack ushered Bob into the very presence of the historical Christ this book is designed to defend. His death is a sober reminder that "*soon* this life will be past—and only what's done for Christ will last." Thus, *The Da Vinci Code: Fact or Fiction?* is dedicated to his memory.

PART ONE

THE Da VINCI DECEPTION

PAUL L. MAIER

A vast double standard overhangs Western society today that is totally deplorable—namely, *you dare not attack any of the religious systems of the world . . . except for Christianity*. To criticize the polytheism and caste system in Hinduism or fault Gautama Buddha for leaving his wife and son to meditate in the forest provokes immediate charges of intolerance and bigotry. To question aspects of the prophet Muhammad's life is not politically correct in a pluralist society—and can even be dangerous.[1] To identify *any* Jewish role whatever in the Good Friday trial of Jesus raises instant charges of anti-Semitism. But skewer Christianity? Caricature Christ and present falsehoods about the church he founded? *No problem*! Join the crowd! It's the "in" thing—politically *very* correct and high fashion to boot!

THE JESUS GAME

The past four decades in particular have seen an outpouring of sensationalist books, motion pictures, and television specials in which Jesus and the true origins of Christianity are barely recognizable. We might call this phenomenon "The Jesus Game," and here is how it is played: Begin with a general sketch of Jesus on the basis of the Gospels, but then distort it as much as you please. Add clashing colors, paint in a bizarre background, and add episodes to the life of Christ that could not possibly have happened. If the end result still faintly resembles the Jesus of the New Testament, you lose. But if you come up with a radically different—and above all, sensational—portrait of Jesus, you win. The prize is maximum coverage in the nation's print and broadcast media. Any frowns from the faithful will be ignored amid the skyrocketing sales of your product.

The Jesus Game has been played ever since the pagan philosopher Celsus first helped set up the rules in the second century AD, but it has never been played with such enthusiasm as at the present moment.

Consider some of the recent players:

- England's Hugh Schonfield unveiled a portrait of Jesus in 1966 that might well be styled "The Passover Plotter"—a false "Savior" who schemed the whole Golgotha scenario.[2]
- Nikos Kazantzakis's book *The Last Temptation of Christ*, later made into a movie, cast Jesus as an object of St. Paul's scorn.[3]
- Also in the tumultuous '60s, we might even have expected to see "Jesus the Radical Revolutionary," courtesy of the S. G. F. Brandon books.[4]
- Of course, there were mercurial (read

"bewildered") authors like John M. Allegro, another British scholar who once worked on the Dead Sea Scrolls but ruined his reputation by favoring us with the image of "Jesus the Mushroom Cultist" in 1970. In his *The Sacred Mushroom and the Cross*, Allegro seriously argued that Jesus was invented by myth-makers who got high on the hallucinogenic qualities of the red-topped, white-flecked fly agaric mushroom and wrote the Gospels to communicate their cultic secrets![5]

- Not to be outdone, Morton Smith presented "Christ the Master Magician" in his 1973 book *The Secret Gospel*, explaining away Jesus' miracles as sleight-of-hand.[6]
- In claims similar to those in the Qur'an, Australian Donovan Joyce's *The Jesus Scroll* unveiled "Jesus the Senescent Savior" who survived Golgotha and lived on to the ripe old age of eighty.[7]
- "Jesus the Happy Husband" staged his debut in several books, the most influential of which was Baigent, Lincoln, and Leigh's *Holy Blood, Holy Grail* in the 1980s.[8] These authors spun the impossible saga that is the heart of the storyline of *The Da Vinci Code*—that Jesus married Mary Magdalene and that their offspring

persisted in the Merovingian dynasty of medieval France.

- After Jesus as "The Clownish Christ" in *Godspell* and "The Rock Redeemer" in *Jesus Christ Superstar* (both forgivable) came the '90s and the irrepressible John Dominic Crossan, oracle of the Jesus Seminar, who gifted us with "Jesus the Rustic Redeemer" (or, perhaps, "Seinfeld—the Savior," depending on which chapter you follow in his *The Historical Jesus—The Life of a Jewish Mediterranean Peasant*).[9]

The television and film media have been quick to follow suit. Whenever one of the networks attempts a serious documentary on Jesus, it usually tips scholarly representation heavily in the direction of radical, revisionist critics rather than serious, centrist biblical scholars, as witness Peter Jennings's ABC special "The Search for Jesus," which aired in June, 2000, or *Dateline NBC* in February, 2004. Bank on it: John Dominic Crossan and his colorful Irish brogue will always have a prominent role on such programs because of his sensationalist attacks on traditional Christianity.

And now, crowning this retinue of revisionism, comes *The Da Vinci Code* by Dan Brown.[10] What sets this latest, horrendously skewed portrait of Jesus apart is not its originality—its central premise, in fact, is just a copy of *Holy Blood, Holy Grail*—but its sales. With multi-millions of copies sold as of this writing, *Da Vinci* enjoys a greater readership than all of the previous books combined, which only compounds the damage done to the cause of truth, as we shall see.

And the damage will continue. The book is being translated into 45 languages worldwide and became a film from Columbia Pictures in May, 2006.

How to explain the novel's success? For openers, "Weird sells," as a colleague who teaches literature commented, wryly. Then, too, Brown and the Doubleday promotion machine, with superb timing, capitalized on the current disenchantment with Roman Catholicism due to the pedophilia and "lavender clergy" scandals, thus aiming at an already vulnerable target. The rise of radical feminism and the women's movement in general was also a powerful assist, as *Newsweek*'s cover story on Mary Magdalene demonstrated (December 8, 2003). In *The Da Vinci Code*, the author claims to restore the feminine role to the place supposedly denied it by male church authorities. Add to that an opening murder inside the Louvre Museum in Paris, a labyrinth of symbolic clues followed by an embattled couple chased by Interpol, and intrigue involving the church, the state, and secret societies, and you have the perfect formula for a page-turner.

A SKILLFUL MYSTERY

Unquestionably, Dan Brown spins a yarn that engrosses the reader. The settings in the museums, cathedrals, and châteaus of France and England are realistic, and some of the detail is well researched. The action is breathtakingly rapid—all 454 pages cover a period measured in hours rather than days or weeks. These pages easily qualify as a thriller for the more intelligent, and those who thrive on mysteries, puzzles, riddles, and enigmas will be quickly hooked. Conspiracy theorists and other fringe sorts, of course, will be riveted, since this is their kind of fare. Beyond debate, the intriguing plot and brisk dialogue are also quite responsible for the book's success.

Not that this novel is in any way "pure genius," as one of the reviewers gushes on the jacket flap.[11] The characters are thin, and the excessively *long* string of clues in the plot finally borders on the tedious, prompting the reader to shout at the printed page toward the close, "Enough, already!"

The novel's ending is also a substantial letdown: we spend over 400 pages searching for the climactic goal to which all the clues are supposed to lead, only to find that goal evaporating before our eyes just as we finally reach it. The anticipated remains of the central figure do not appear, nor do the trunks crammed with the "Sangreal documents" supposedly proving the significance of those remains. One has the impression that the author, having exhausted the twists and turns of his complicated plot, has simply run out of story and elected to tie up any loose ends quickly and escape.

On the other hand, who can quarrel with success? Literally millions of readers are finding *The Da Vinci Code* compelling reading. But one thing is very clear: this novel could never have succeeded simply as a good mystery without Brown's gratuitous broadsides against Christianity. His sensationalist claims may not have been necessary for the central story line, but they were certainly essential in the eyes of a conspiracy-happy public. To this his fans might quickly respond, "Hey, lighten up! It's *only fiction* after all!" But when fiction is peddled as fact, it becomes more than a mere story and raises the potential for great harm.

WHEN FICTION BECOMES FACT

Be it said to Brown's credit: the literary category for *Da Vinci* is fiction indeed, whereas the list of Jesus-caricature books mentioned previously—though intrinsically fictional—had the audacity to be published as nonfiction. Provisionally, this puts Brown a cut above the previous authors—though not for long.

The art of successful fiction is to engender in the reader a sense of total reality, so that what the person is reading seems true, like something actually happening to real people in real situations. To be sure, when a reader comes to the end of a chapter and puts the book down, this suspension of disbelief is interrupted for a time, only to be quickly restored at the next reading. Add to that phenomenon the fact that every reader anticipates—justifiably—that *all information in the context of the novel is actually true* even though the main characters may be fictional, and the result is that fiction becomes fact for too many readers.

Apparently, this is especially true in the case of religious novels and theological thrillers. Some years ago, when Taylor Caldwell's highly imaginative novel on St. Paul, *Great Lion of God*, was published, I regularly had to field serious questions from her readers about details in the life of St. Paul *that she had invented out of thin air*![12] One memorable query was this: "Is it true that St. Paul, as a teenager, was seduced by a Syrian slave girl in a meadow near Antioch, and that explains his attitude toward women? Why didn't my pastor ever tell me that?" I think my "*No! Never!*" was accompanied by steam jetting out of my ears.

This is why *The Da Vinci Code* is so dangerous. Many readers assume that all of the supplementary contextual and background detail involving Christianity is true *when it is not*. Rather, the few factual references are heavily interlaced with fiction or outright falsehood. To represent such details as fact is positively dishonest. Yet Brown does exactly this, starting on the very first page, where, under the heading of "FACT," he presents opening statements that form the basis of the entire novel. Furthermore, Brown has publicly clarified that he believes that the conspiracy theory he presents in the *The Da Vinci Code* is actually true.[13]

In all direct quotations from the novel that follow, the views presented are unquestionably those of Brown himself, since the reader is led to assume full credibility in the dialogue of all the major personalities in the book. Identifying the speaker in each case, therefore, is unnecessary, although the majority of the misstatements throughout the novel may be attributed to a character named Leigh Teabing (Leigh plus Baigent—the anagram of Teabing—are two of the three authors of *Holy Blood, Holy Grail*, which is the source for the main plot line in *Da Vinci*).

The Priory of Sion

Even before the novel gets underway we see this blend of fact and fiction. In the same prefatory list of "facts" as above, Brown places the Vatican prelature known as Opus Dei cheek by jowl with "The Priory of Sion." Both groups play very central roles in this novel, Opus Dei that of the antagonists and the Priory those heroic sorts who secretly communicate the truth about Jesus and the early church. But while Opus Dei is indeed an authentic, fiercely conservative, Roman Catholic organization, the Priory merits no credibility whatever.

"The Priory of Sion" is supposedly a secret European society founded in Jerusalem in 1099 by a crusading French king named Godefroi de Bouillon (in fact, 1956 is the true date, and it was officially registered in France). Its purpose, according to Brown, was to preserve a great secret that had been handed down from generation to generation of Godefroi's ancestors since the time of Christ. Hidden documents buried beneath the ruins of the Temple in Jerusalem allegedly corroborated this secret. And what was the "great secret" that they supposedly sheltered? Jesus' marriage to Mary Magdalene, which resulted in a daughter named Sarah. Jesus' bloodline supposedly continued through the Merovingian dynasty of French kings and survives even today. The Priory of Sion exists, Brown claims, to keep a watchful eye over the descendants of Jesus and Mary and wait for the perfect moment to reveal the secret to the world.

Search for the Priory of Sion at a university library and you will likely find little or nothing. Switch to the Internet—that egalitarian haven for both sages and charlatans—and you will find yourself trudging through a wilderness of the bizarre, the occult, and the weird, a general electronic gathering ground for devotees of New Age esoterica and fanatics of the fringe. One reliable title does appear on the search engine: "The Priory of Sion *Hoax.*" To claim that this group gained the allegiance of past greats such as Sandro Botticelli, Leonardo da Vinci, and Isaac Newton is actually an assault on their respective memories and reputations.

The Priory's role in this novel is supposedly "proven" by a cache of documents that were discovered in the Bibliotheque Nationale in Paris. These documents really do exist, but they were planted there by a forger named Pierre Plantard. In fact, one of Plantard's henchmen admitted to assisting him in the fabrication of these materials, including the genealogical tables and lists of the Priory's grand masters—all trumpeted as truth in *The Da Vinci Code*. Plantard's hoax was actually exposed in a series of French books and a BBC documentary in 1996, but this news—fortunately for Dan Brown—is reaching our shores only at glacial speed. Plantard turned out to be an anti-Semite with a criminal record for fraud, while the real Priory of Sion is a little splinter social group founded half a century ago.[14] The most important strand in the central plot of *The Da Vinci Code*, then, is a total hoax. So much for the "Fact" Brown claims on his first page!

Calumny against Constantine

Next we have the most concerted falsification of a historical personality that I have ever encountered in either fiction or nonfiction. The victim is Constantine, the first Christian Roman emperor. Writes Brown: "The Priory believes that Constantine and his male successors successfully converted the world from matriarchal paganism to patriarchal Christianity by waging a campaign of propaganda that demonized the sacred feminine, obliterating the goddess from modern religion forever" (page 124).

The author claims that Constantine not only eliminated goddess worship in the Roman Empire, he also collated the Bible, used Christianity for political gain, moved Christian worship from Saturday to Sunday, and decided that Jesus should be made into a deity in order to suit his own purposes. In reality, the first Christian emperor did many things for church and society in the early fourth century, but *not one* of these claims is among them.

According to Brown's character Leigh Teabing, Constantine "commissioned and financed a new Bible, which omitted those gospels that spoke of Christ's *human* traits and embellished those gospels that made him godlike" (234). *False!* Most of the canon was well known and in use nearly two centuries *before* Constantine, a time when the early church had already dismissed the many apocryphal gospels that arose later in the second century. The rejected gospels, far from containing the real truth about Jesus, were all distortions derived from the first-century canonical Gospels and laced with fanciful aberrations.[15]

For Brown, Constantine "was a lifelong pagan who was baptized on his deathbed, too weak to protest" (232). This assertion is also totally false. While Constantine was undeniably a flawed individual, historians agree that he certainly abjured paganism, became a genuine Christian convert, repaid the church for its terrible losses during the persecutions, favored the clergy, built many churches throughout his empire, convened the first ecumenical council at Nicea—underwriting the expenses of clergy to attend it—and *desired* baptism near death. As for the last, he was merely following the custom at the time (innocent though mistaken) of delaying baptism until the end of life because it wiped your slate clean of preceding sins.[16]

Did Constantine shift Christian worship from Saturday to Sunday "to coincide with the pagan's veneration day of the sun" (232–233). No. The earliest Christians started worshiping on the first day of the week, Sunday, which they called "the Lord's Day," to honor the day on which Christ rose from the dead. This is obvious both from the New Testament (Acts 20:7, 1 Corinthians 16:2,

Revelation 1:10), as well as in the writings of the earliest church fathers, among them Ignatius of Antioch, Justin Martyr, the *Didache*, and even the pagan author Pliny the Younger.[17]

The Council of Nicea, in Brown's revisionism, deified Jesus. Before that, "Jesus was viewed by His followers as a mortal prophet . . . a great and powerful man, but a *man* nonetheless," not the Son of God (233). Once again, Brown's premise is utterly mistaken. Jesus' deity was attested by many New Testament passages, as well as by the earliest Christians and all the church fathers, even if there was some disagreement as to the precise nature of that deity. The Council of Nicea did not debate over whether Jesus was divine or only mortal, but whether he was coeternal with the Father.

Still, it was by "a relatively close vote" that the Council of Nicea endorsed Jesus' deity, claims Brown (233). In fact, the vote was 300 to 2![18] Constantine, then, is the target for some of Brown's most outrageous offenses against history in his battle with the truth.

Did Jesus Wed Mary Magdalene?

Having painted a Constantine that his own mother, Helena, would not have recognized, Brown moves on to Mary Magdalene, who has always been *the* prime candidate for the role of "Mrs. Jesus." Writes Brown:

> "The early Church needed to convince the world that the mortal prophet Jesus was a divine being. Therefore, any gospels that described earthly aspects of Jesus' life had to be omitted from the Bible. Unfortunately for the early editors, one particularly troubling earthly theme kept recurring in the gospels. Mary Magdalene. . . . More specifically, her marriage to Jesus Christ. . . . It's a matter of historical record" (244).

In sober fact, Jesus never wed anyone, but for years sensationalizing scholars and their novelistic popularizers have played the role of doting mothers trying to marry off an eligible son. Now, if there were even one *spark* of evidence from antiquity that Jesus even *may* have gotten married, then as a historian, I would have to weigh this evidence against the *total* absence of such information in either Scripture or the early church traditions. But there is no such spark—not a scintilla of evidence—anywhere in historical sources. Even where one might expect to find such claims in the bizarre, second-century, apocryphal gospels—which the Jesus Seminar and other radical voices are trying so desperately to rehabilitate—there is no reference that Jesus ever got married.

Not to be frustrated by anything as fragile as truth, however, sensationalizing authors insist on the contrary. One of them presented as "proof" of Jesus' marriage the fact that Jewish men were expected to marry, according to rabbinical tradition. This "evidence" plays a major role in Dan Brown's Jesus-as-husband theory as well. Yet it is a logical error to claim that Jesus could not have remained single because of a general expectation of marriage. Furthermore, exceptions for bachelorhood were granted by the rabbis, and there were whole sub-groups in Judaism that practiced celibacy, such as a branch of the Essenes or the Egyptian Therapeutae familiar from Philo. Nor did many of the great prophets, such as Jeremiah, or the wilderness prophet Banus—under whom Josephus studied—or John the Baptist, have wives. Jesus was regularly linked with such as a desert prophet early in his ministry.

Nevertheless, we now have endless variations on the theme of Jesus' marriage to Mary Magdalene, and then, of course, their child or children come along as well. In *Holy Blood, Holy Grail*—the source of many of the theories presented in *The Da Vinci Code*—Mary, pregnant with Jesus' child, fled to France, where she gave birth to a girl named Sarah, who became an ancestress of the Merovingian dynasty in France. Do these allegations come from early, original sources? Hardly; this version of Jesus' family life first surfaced in the ninth century AD.

Brown doesn't stop with the borrowed theory

of Jesus as husband and father but continues with further bizarre claims:

> "Jesus was the original feminist. He intended for the future of His Church to be in the hands of Mary Magdalene. . . . She was of the House of Benjamin . . . of royal descent" (248).

In fact, there is no record whatever of Mary's Jewish tribal affiliation, nor of a member in the tribe of Benjamin thereby having royal blood. And there is nothing to suggest that Jesus commissioned Mary instead of the apostles as the original church leader.

The cornerstone of Brown's "evidence" for Jesus' marriage to Mary Magdalene comes from the apocryphal *Gospel of Philip.* Crucial segments of the passage Brown will cite are missing in the manuscript, since the first line actually reads: "And the companion of . . . Mary Magdalene . . . her more than the disciples . . . kiss her . . ." Yet Brown bravely translates the subject as Jesus (who, by the way, may have kissed only *her hand*). And "companion," Brown renders as "spouse or wife in Aramaic":

> And the companion of the Saviour is Mary Magdalene. Christ loved her more than all the disciples and used to kiss her

> often on her mouth. The rest of the disciples were offended by it and expressed disapproval. They said to him, "Why do you love her more than all of us?" (246)

This supposedly airtight proof breaks down immediately. If Jesus had a wife, it would have been unthinkable for his disciples to speak out against her, no matter how strong their disapproval. And Brown commits a further blunder here: the *Gospel of Philip* was not written in Aramaic, as he claims, but in Greek. And *Philip* is very late among the apocryphal gospels, dating to the third century, at least two centuries removed from Jesus' time. Scholars dismiss the work as having no genuine historical recollections that are not drawn from the canonical Gospels. Not only is it one of the late Gnostic apocryphal writings that the early church rejected, but it is apocryphal also in the literal understanding of that term today: "not genuine, spurious, counterfeit."

The same is true of the other document that Brown references in support of his married-Jesus hypothesis, the *Gospel of Mary Magdalene*, which is also too late for credibility. And even if these two writings *were* authentic, neither specifies that Jesus was actually married. And yet Brown's character Teabing shamelessly exaggerates, "I shan't bore you with the countless references to Jesus and Magdalene's union" (247). But such references can indeed be counted: there are *only two*! Both are late, and even they do not explicitly report any "union" of Jesus and Mary!

Why is there no record whatever of Jesus' marriage in all of church history? Dan Brown, echoing other revisionist authors before him, claims that the church suppressed this evidence in a great conspiracy of silence. This, of course, raises the antennae of conspiracy-lovers everywhere, the sorts who thrive on UFO sightings and alien invasions from outer space and who fear the Tri-Lateral Commission. "Everyone loves a conspiracy," writes Brown, knowingly, and clearly, many do. For this reason he can get away with the outrageous lie that Jesus' marriage is "a matter of historical record" (244). The reality: No history. No record.

While we do not have one *wisp* of historical evidence that Jesus ever married, we do have *powerful* evidence that he did *not*. Even the most radical revisionists agree with sober biblical scholars that the writings of St. Paul constitute our earliest—and therefore most credible—records of Christianity. In 1 Corinthians 9:5, Paul defended his right to have a wife—a prerogative he never implemented: "Do we not have the right to be accompanied by a wife, as the other apostles, and the brothers of the Lord and Cephas [Peter]?" Now if Jesus himself had ever married, Paul would *surely* have cited that as the greatest precedent of all, after which it would have been unnecessary even to mention such subordinate examples as Peter and the other apostles. Without question, 1 Corinthians 9:5 is the graveyard of the married-Jesus fiction.

But what if there *were* some real piece of evidence for Jesus' marriage? One can hardly resist speculating as to whether Jesus' mission to the world would have been compromised had he, in fact, wed. Certainly entering into marriage, as ordained by God, is not sinful, so might not Christ have done so? The *Da Vinci* heroine, for example, claims she would "have no problem" with a married Jesus, and many readers might agree. But one of the principal purposes of marriage is to have children, and an enormous—even cosmic—problem would have arisen if Jesus and the Magdalene *had* produced offspring. Theologians would have argued for centuries as to whether such children did or did not participate in Jesus' divinity. And what of their children and grandchildren in turn? It would have caused no less than theological bedlam. That Christ remained celibate was very wise indeed!

The Knights Templar

According to Brown and his sensationalist sources, the church suppressed the secret of Jesus' marriage to Mary Magdalene. Yet the "secret" would not die. To guard and convey that secret and to retrieve the Sangreal documents that corroborated it from under the Jerusalem Temple, the Priory of Sion supposedly created the oldest of the church's military-religious orders: the Knights Templar.

Born during the Crusades to protect pilgrims on their way to and from the Holy Land, the Knights were indeed founded in 1118 and should have become obsolete when the last Crusader fortress at Acre fell in 1291. But by then they had amassed considerable wealth and had metamorphosed into a medieval banking institution cum travel agency. Thus far, the facts.[19]

But in Brown's rewrite of history, the Templars were supposedly suppressed by Pope Clement V because they were blackmailing him with the secret of the Holy Grail. (That symbol of the ideal unattainable is one of history's most elusive and protean objects of human quest, variously defined as anything from the cup Jesus used at the Last Supper to the Shroud of Turin.) Borrowing from *Holy Blood, Holy Grail*, Brown divides the term *Sangreal* (Medieval French for Holy Grail) into *Sang* (blood) and *Real* (royal). That royal blood, in Brown's story, is the bloodline stemming from Jesus and Mary Magdalene through the Merovingian dynasty. Mary herself was the actual Holy Grail, "the chalice that bore the royal bloodline of Jesus Christ" (249). The Templars knew that this formidable secret, if revealed, could undermine both papacy and church, so they used their knowledge for political gain. Rather than submit to blackmail, Pope Clement V devised his "ingeniously planned sting operation" (159), arrested all the Templars, and burned them as heretics. Thus far, the fiction.

In sober fact, it was King Philip IV ("the Fair") of France who, desperate for the Templars' wealth, forced the pope to suppress their order, whereupon the French king—not the pope—arrested them and burned some, including Grand Master Jacques de Molay, at the stake in 1314.

With the Templars terminated, who would guard the great secret? Its original custodians, of course, the Priory of Sion, that latter-day group with invented roots going back to the Templars. Indeed, the Priory, according to Brown,

> ". . . to this day still worships Mary Magdalene as the Goddess, the Holy Grail, the Rose, and the Divine Mother. . . . [She] was pregnant at the time of the crucifixion. For the safety of Christ's unborn child, she had no choice but to flee the Holy Land. With the help of Jesus' trusted uncle, Joseph of Arimathea, Mary Magdalene secretly traveled to France, then known as Gaul. There she found safe refuge in the Jewish community. It

> was here in France that she gave birth to a daughter. Her name was Sarah." *(255)*

But enough of such fables. We have already discussed the true origins of the Priory of Sion and the baseless nature of the idea that Jesus was married; here we will simply note the fact that Joseph of Arimathea was *not* Jesus' uncle.

The Sacred Feminine

Matriarchal paganism, that pristine faith presumably suppressed by "patriarchal Christianity," seems to be the secret spiritual ideal Brown advocates throughout *The Da Vinci Code*. In his view there should be, in place of God or beside him, a consort goddess worthy of equal or even superior worship. Such a concept finds ready resonance among radical feminist theologians today, some of whom are urging a reappraisal of Sophia, the supreme goddess of second-century Gnosticism. Without detouring into that hydra-headed Christian heresy, one might well question instead the ethics associated with Brown's crusade on behalf of the sacred feminine. Here we find no lofty idealism to support the distaff side of divinity but rather a lusty advocacy of free sexual indulgence as part of a worship unfettered by Judeo-Christian principles.

According to Brown, the church "demonized

sex," whereas those favoring the sacred feminine regard it as a quasi-sacrament. As witness to this, Brown depicts a lurid ritual he painted directly out of the film *Eyes Wide Shut*. The scene shows a circle of costumed men and women devotees offering up a weird chant in a nocturnal, candlelit cellar as they surround a copulating couple in the center. At least Brown's heroine has the decency to be scandalized by the scene (until it is all explained to her in the end), but the ultimate message to the reader is this: it may *look* bad, but it's really okay because this is *hieros gamos*, a "holy marriage" rite associated with the sacred feminine. The endless references in this book to Aphrodite or Venus—for whom Brown finds impossible symbolism everywhere from planetary movements to Walt Disney productions—only reinforce this theme.

In fact, far from "demonizing sex," Christianity regards sexuality as one of God's greatest gifts—albeit a gift that should be used responsibly. In this scary era of venereal disease, HIV, herpes, and other sexually transmitted diseases, this view is hardly outdated. The libertinism suggested in *The Da Vinci Code* would only exacerbate the dangers brought about by the Sexual Revolution. Nor has any mainstream religious system ever placed women on a higher plane than Christianity. The target for Brown's feminist crusade should instead have been those current major religions that have *not* yet experienced the blessings of women's liberation.

Revising Art and Music

Brown also moves his revisionism into the world of art, for he claims that it was Leonardo da Vinci himself who, in painting *The Last Supper*, surfaced the great secret for all who had eyes to see. "*The Last Supper* practically shouts at the viewer that Jesus and Magdalene were a pair" (244). Admittedly, the apostle John, at Jesus' right hand, does have a feminine look to him in Da Vinci's masterpiece, but that was the master's habit in painting younger men, as witness his portrayals also of John the Baptist and others. Moreover, the great artist could not possibly have had Mary Magdalene in mind or there would have been *fourteen* figures in his fresco, rather than Jesus and the Twelve. If the figure at Jesus' right hand *is* the Magdalene, where is the missing John?

As for Leonardo's *Mona Lisa* ("La Gioconda"), it is *not* an androgynous self-portrait, as Brown claims, but an actual portrait of a real personality, Madonna Lisa, the wife of Francesco del Giocondo. Her "secret smile" does not derive from her name, which is supposedly an anagram of two Egyptian fertility deities Amon and Isis in Brown's *faux* entry into art (121).[20]

Nor is music exempt from such revisionism.

Brown writes that Richard Wagner's opera *Parsifal* "was a tribute to Mary Magdalene and the bloodline of Jesus Christ, told through the story of a young knight on a quest for truth" (390). The young knight in the opera is indeed on a quest for the Holy Grail—the traditional Grail, that is, not its redefinition in this novel.

Restructuring Architecture

The Da Vinci Code's excursion into Gothic architecture must have had Sigmund Freud as the tour guide. Brown claims, via Teabing, that the Priory of Sion attached female sexual symbolism to the medieval cathedrals to represent goddess worship, an idea that would have enraged the original architects, who had nothing of the sort in mind. According to Brown, the "cathedral's long hollow nave" is "a secret tribute to a woman's womb . . . complete with receding labial ridges and a nice little cinquefoil clitoris above the doorway" (326).

But neither the nebulous Priory nor the Templars had anything to do with medieval cathedral architecture. The great churches of Europe not only predated them by centuries, but they generally have *three* doors at their main entrances rather than one, plus further doors in the side transepts. Thus, the parallel with a woman's body becomes difficult to fathom.

Had Brown read studies on the architectural history of medieval cathedrals rather than the maunderings of sensationalists, he would have learned that both the later Gothic and earlier Romanesque structures derived their "long hollow nave" from the public basilicas of the ancient Greco-Roman world.

Distortions on Display

Other endearing phrases in the book include "the New Testament is based on fabrications" (341); "the greatest story ever told is, in fact, the greatest story ever *sold*" (267); and "the Church has two thousand years of experience pressuring those who threaten to unveil its lies" (407). The anti-Christian bias of the author is obvious and blatant. This is certainly not to say that the Church has always been on the side of the angels. Anything but! It has committed many tragic errors across the centuries, including medieval anti-Semitism, the Crusades, the Inquisition, the Galileo affair, and other persecutions. And just look at the evils perpetrated today by the few members of the clergy who inflict on children the horrors of pedophilia. But keeping "Jesus' marriage to Mary Magdalene" under wraps—the main theme in Brown's book—is not one of the church's offenses.

Detailing all of the errors, misinterpretations, deceptions, distortions, and outright falsehoods in

The Da Vinci Code makes one wonder whether Brown's manuscript ever underwent editorial scrutiny or fact-checking. The entire novel is literally riddled with miscues, the most important and obvious of which we shall examine here. For purposes of clarity, Brown's statements, in bold print, will precede each instance. All are direct quotes.

"Noah was himself an albino" (166). There is no canonical evidence for this. And the "albino monk" of Opus Dei seems to have no problem whatever with his eyesight, as would be the case with true albinism. Besides all of which, Opus Dei does not have an order of monks. Nor does it have a bishop, as claimed for one of Brown's central characters.

"The early Jewish tradition involved ritualistic sex. *In the Temple, no less.* Early Jews believed that the Holy of Holies in Solomon's Temple housed not only God but also His powerful female equal, Shekinah" (309). This atrocious claim provokes either dismissive laughter or head-shakings of stupefaction among biblical scholars, for it is a ridiculous assertion based on fantasy rather than fact. Nothing was—or is—as basic to the Hebrews as their foundational belief in *one* God (not two or more); monotheism is the ancient Jews' great gift to the world. Attaching sexuality of any kind to this *one* God was so abhorrent to Jews that they did not even have a word in

Hebrew for *goddess*. The term "Shekinah" in Hebrew refers to the glory of God present in his indwelling, not some divine consort.

"The Jewish tetragrammaton YHWH—the sacred name of God—in fact derived from Jehovah, an androgynous physical union between the masculine *Jah* and the pre-Hebraic name for Eve, *Havah*" (309). False in its entirety! YHWH, the original name for God, reflects the Hebrew verb "to be." But since tradition forbade verbal pronunciation of the name, rabbis in the sixteenth century pronounced the consonants from YHWH together with the vowels from the word *Adonai* ("Lord") resulting in the word "Jehovah." This *later*, synthesized name not only did not predate YHWH, it has absolutely nothing to do with an androgynous union.

"As a tribute to the magic of Venus, the Greeks used her eight-year cycle to organize their Olympic Games" (36). Here Brown shows himself to be an equal-opportunity exploiter in his crusade against the truth, muddling Greek history as well as Jewish and Christian history. In reality, the games were dedicated to Zeus. A day-long festival in his honor interrupted the games midway through, which is why they were terminated in the Christian era until their revival in 1896 on a strictly secular basis. They also occurred every four years rather than eight, as Brown implies. As for the five linked rings of the Olympic flag in the modern games, these had nothing to do with the "Ishtar pentagram," since new rings were supposed to be added with each new set of games. The organizers, however, stopped at five—a nice number to fill Olympic logos, reflecting the five major, inhabited continents.[21]

"The Bible . . . has evolved through countless translations, additions, and revisions. History has never had a definitive version of the book" (231). To say that the Bible has "evolved" implies a progression of constant change, as in the term *evolution.* This is totally misleading. The only "changes" to the Bible that have taken place across the centuries have been an ever-more-faithful rendering and translation of the original Hebrew of the Old Testament and the Greek of the New Testament, without *any* additions to the text. Part 2 will discuss this matter in further detail.

"More than *eighty* gospels were considered for the New Testament, and yet only a relative few were chosen for inclusion" (231). Brown's statement implies that there was a general submission of gospels to some sort of early church panel that reduced the field to the familiar four. This was not at all the case. Matthew, Mark, Luke, and John were foundation documents in what later came to be called the New Testament. Eusebius, the first church historian, tells how they were the core of the canon from the start, and how their authority was determined on the basis of *usage* in such early Christian centers as Jerusalem, Antioch, Alexandria, and Rome. He also clearly identifies some of the later spurious writings, including the Gnostic gospels, that the church rejected as soon as they surfaced.[22] Today they are known as the "New Testament apocrypha." Brown must have had this group in mind with his "eighty," which is an exaggerated figure in any case.

Speaking of exaggeration, Brown outdoes himself in the following: **"Because Constantine upgraded Jesus' status almost four centuries *after* Jesus' death, thousands of documents already existed chronicling His life as a *mortal* man"** (234). First of all, Constantine did not "upgrade Jesus' status." The New Testament makes it clear that the earliest Christians regarded Jesus as divine. Furthermore, since Jesus died in AD 33 and Constantine converted in AD 312, almost *three* (not four) centuries is the proper time span. But did "thousands of documents" exist regarding Jesus as a mortal? Sorry. Try several dozen instead, which tell not only of his mortal humanity but his divinity as well!

"The Sangreal documents include tens of thousands of pages of information. . . . in four enormous trunks. . . . that the Knights Templar found under Solomon's Temple" (256).

In fact, there was no such find. No trunks, no documents, nor even any search for them by the Knights Templar. Furthermore, the Jerusalem Temple—the very citadel of Judaism—would be the last place on earth to look for *Christian* documents relating to the Holy Grail. And even in fiction, Brown cannot produce these "tens of thousands of pages" for us at the culmination of his plot.

"Fortunately for historians . . . some of the gospels that Constantine attempted to eradicate managed to survive. The Dead Sea Scrolls were found in the 1950s hidden in a cave near Qumran in the Judean desert" (234). Here we have three serious errors in less than three lines. Constantine, of course, was not in the business of eradicating any gospels. The Dead Sea Scrolls were discovered in 1947, not the 1950s. And they did not contain any gospels or any references to Jesus.

"Of course, the Vatican . . . tried very hard to suppress the release of these Scrolls" (234). This malicious but tired old canard, so popular among conspiracy theorists and sensationalist authors, is disproved by the numerous publications of Scroll translations. None of the Scrolls involves Christianity. They do, however, prove the accuracy of manuscript recopying of the Old Testament and show a thought world very similar to that portrayed in the Gospel of John. In other words, the Vatican would—and does—regard them as very congenial to the faith and by no means antagonistic.

"The Merovingians founded Paris" (257). In fact, the city was already well established about seven centuries before they arrived.[23]

"Dagobert was a Merovingian king . . . stabbed in the eye while sleeping . . . Assassinated by the Vatican in collusion with Pepin d'Heristal" (257–258). No. Dagobert, while hunting in a forest, was murdered by one of his companions who had been suborned by Ebroin, mayor of the palace of Neustria—thus, not while sleeping, not by the Vatican, and not "in collusion with Pepin d'Heristal."[24] While one may object that this is quibbling over pedantic detail, Brown's continual attacks on Catholicism—most of them unjustified—should be exposed for what they are. And incidentally, "the Vatican" could hardly have been involved in his murder, since the Roman Catholic Church headquarters in those days were at the Lateran Palace, not the Vatican.

"During 300 years of witch hunts, the Church burned at the stake an astonishing five *million* women" (125). While even *one* woman burned during the European witch craze was a horror unto itself and never justifiable, in sober fact the number was between 30,000 and 50,000 victims, according to historians. Not all were women, not all were terminated in that fashion, and the executing agent was often the state or private individuals rather than the church.[25]

"Tarot had been devised as a secret means to pass along ideologies banned by the Church" (92). Nothing of the sort. They appeared in the fifteenth century as nothing more than playing cards and did not take on significance related to the occult until the late eighteenth.

Brown's other miscues are of less importance, even if they also deviate from the facts in every instance.

Well, there it is: according to *The Da Vinci Code*, Christianity was built on a lie, but pagan polytheism and goddess worship were structured on the truth! Without question, Dan Brown has played "The Jesus Game" as a winner.

WHY NOT TRY THE TRUTH?

All such Jesus Game players and their caricatures of Christ have the following in common:

1. The flight from hard evidence—solid historical, literary, and archaeological source material—to the flimsies of sensationalistic reconstruction.
2. The substitution of opinion for fact and hypothesis for history, leading to the most arbitrary conclusions possible.

3. Twisting the language of a historical source out of context to make it mean what the author wants it to mean in accord with his caricature.
4. Exchanging objectivity for bias, admitting only sources that favor the author's hypothesis and dismissing the rest.
5. What might be called "smorgasbord research": ignoring the succulent dishes of evidence spread out by the past but pouncing on a caviar wisp of data, then reporting that the entire dinner consisted only of delicious fish eggs.
6. Façade "scholarship": peppering the findings with references, book titles, or notes that may look authoritatative, but substantiate nothing at all.
7. In the case of fiction, exaggerating at will, removing data out of context, and masking outright falsehoods under the claim that the literary vehicle is fiction.

Against this misuse of history, the truth has an enormous freshness and credibility. The genuine historical records about Jesus and Christianity are clear, coherent, convincing, and infinitely more credible than the many strands of gossamer gossip that critics and fantasists have spun out to try to occlude them. Quite apart from the copious detail found inside the New Testament, many purely secular sources readily confirm many of the main facts about the life of Christ and the early church. Often the same people, places, and events referenced inside Scripture are cited also in nonbiblical materials. These range from a myriad of geographical place names to the hard evidence provided by archaeology to a host of documents that have come down to us from the ancient world that correlate completely with the biblical evidence.

As for the early church, both the primary sources in the writings of the early fathers and the detailed history of the church's first three centuries by Eusebius of Caesarea provide a quick corrective to the sensationalism foisted on the world by players of "The Jesus Game" today. Even secular history provides a reliable sounding board against which to compare later suppositions about the true history of Christianity.

A CLOSING COMPARISON

Listing errors in a work of literature is not a happy task, and it can even lull the reader into disregarding the perils of the printed page. In concluding, therefore, perhaps a model or analogy of how seriously *The Da Vinci Code* attacks Christianity may be appropriate.

Imagine that someone were to write a novel

about George Washington, the nation's founder, rather than Jesus Christ, the church's founder. At the start, the author assures the reader that all his material is based on fact, then goes on to present the following scenario:

While doing research at Mount Vernon into the life of the father of our country, a veteran scholar is murdered. While dying, he leaves a long trail of intricate clues for his granddaughter and a friend so that they might avenge his death. After solving the clues despite their Byzantine complexity, the two finally learn an awful truth: George Washington was really a member of a secret society that worshiped King George III of England and his queen, Charlotte Sophia. In fact, the reason for the American reverses early in the Revolutionary War was that Washington, a true but clandestine Tory, was secretly communicating Colonial war plans to the British via Benedict Arnold, Washington's secret illegitimate son. At Yorktown, while awaiting a British support fleet, Washington was preparing to surrender to Cornwallis, but when De Grasse arrived with his fleet of French ships to aid the American side, Washington had to accept Cornwallis's surrender instead.

At the end of his life, Washington's conscience got the better of him, and he wrote a confession that was buried with him in his tomb at Mount Vernon. The scholar who discovered it was then murdered by the CIA, who feared that his find would destroy the patriotic mystique of America's founding father and demoralize the country. When the FBI and CIA learn that the granddaughter and her friend know the awful truth, an all-points bulletin is issued for the pair. After a harrowing series of misadventures, the two escape capture. But no, they will not reveal the "truth" about Washington either.

Readers with only a smattering of knowledge about American history but a great appetite for conspiracy might well buy into such worthless madness, since it contains just enough tangential truth—real people, real places, real situations—to be credible. While the parallel with *The Da Vinci Code* is certainly imperfect, Dan Brown has accomplished a very similar hoax, successful largely because so many today have "only a smattering of knowledge" about Jesus and Christianity.

ULTIMATE TRUTH

Can it be that Dan Brown truly believes his own aberrant misconstructions, as he has claimed? Or is he, perhaps, post-Modernist in his philosophy? Such deconstructionists believe that "whatever is true for you is the truth, pure and simple; there are no objective standards or universal norms, since everything is relative." Even as I write, they are attempting to ruin the historical disciplines and have apparently widened their target to include literature as well (actually, literature may well be the place where post-Modernism started: "Forget whatever truth the author was trying to convey—accept only what seems true to you").

I, for one, would hate to be treated in a hospital in which the doctors could prescribe whatever struck their momentary fancy as a medical necessity ("I know he has an appendicitis, but I'd prefer doing a tonsilectomy this morning"). And would anyone fly in a plane whose pilots chose an altitude based on their current high or low moods?

Truth is truer than any subjective assaults on it, regardless of whatever may be the whim of the moment. Several times in his novel, Brown avers, "Everyone loves a conspiracy." One can only hope that, at the end of the day, "everyone" has a final, higher love for the truth.

On a personal basis, I find *The Da Vinci Code* a font of malicious misinformation both as a historian and as a Christian. As a Christian, I am *much* less concerned—the church has been under attack for two millennia and will survive very well indeed, thank you. As a historian, however, I am infuriated when known and universally accepted facts of the past are misrepresented, distorted, or utterly falsified. To all who think, "where there's smoke, there must be some fire" of truth, know that no historian anywhere in the world has endorsed such perversions of the past.

PART TWO

BUT WHAT IS TRUTH?

HANK HANEGRAAFF

"What is truth?" This is the very question Pontius Pilate asked Jesus. In the irony of the ages, the Roman governor stood toe-to-toe with Truth and yet missed its reality. Many people in our postmodern culture are in much the same position. They stare at truth but fail to recognize its identity. So what is truth? The answer is simple: truth is anything that corresponds to reality. As such, truth is not determined by the popularity of a book like *The Da Vinci Code*. Nor is it a matter of preference or opinion. Truth is true even if everyone denies it, and a lie is a lie even if everyone affirms it. When sophistry, sensationalism, and superstition sabotage truth, our view of reality is seriously skewed.

That is precisely what *The Da Vinci Code* does. It is based on an idiosyncratic brand of fundamentalism that is fond of making dogmatic assertions while failing to provide defensible arguments.

We have already seen in the previous section the many reasons why *The Da Vinci Code* can be safely labeled absolute fiction. But demonstrating the falsity of Brown's dogmatic assertions is not the same thing as positively demonstrating the truth of Christianity. The fact that Brown's assertions are based on false faith does not in and of itself prove that the Christian faith is based on the foundation of firm facts. Thus, we now move on to demonstrate what we *know* to be truth—

namely, that the Bible is not merely human but divine in origin, that Jesus Christ is God in human flesh, and that amid the religions of the ancient world, Christianity is demonstrably unique.

GOSPEL TRUTH OR GHASTLY TALES?

The Bible is a product of man, my dear.
Not of God. . . . it has evolved through countless translations, additions, and revisions.
—*The Da Vinci Code*, PAGE 231

Dan Brown is quick to accuse the Bible of being patently unreliable. According to *The Da Vinci Code*, the Bible we have today is merely a copy of a copy of a copy, with fresh errors introduced during each stage of the process. That, however, is far from true. Though we no longer have the original autographs, we can be certain that the copies we have are faithful representations of those original writings.

Manuscript Evidence

First, we should note that the New Testament manuscripts Brown calls into question have stronger manuscript support than any other work of classical literature, including Homer, Plato, Aristotle, Caesar, and Tacitus. There are presently more than five thousand copies of Greek manuscripts in existence[1] and as many as twenty thousand more translations in such languages as Latin, Coptic, and Syriac. Incredibly, there's reason to believe that the earliest manuscript fragments may be dated all the way back to the second half of the first century.[2] This is amazing when you consider that only seven of Plato's manuscripts are in existence today—and there is a 1,300-year gap separating the earliest copy from the original writing! Equally amazing is the fact that the New Testament has been virtually unaltered, as has been documented by scholars who have compared the earliest written manuscripts with copies of manuscripts dated centuries later.

Furthermore, the reliability of the Gospel accounts is confirmed through the eyewitness credentials of the authors. For example, Luke says that he gathered eyewitness testimony and "carefully investigated everything" (Luke 1:1-3). John writes, "That which was from the beginning, which we have heard, which we have seen with our eyes, which we have looked at and our hands have touched—this we proclaim concerning the Word of life" (1 John 1:1). Likewise, the apostle Peter reminded his readers that the disciples "did not follow cleverly invented stories" but "were eyewitnesses of [Jesus'] majesty" (2 Peter 1:16).

Finally, secular historians—including Josephus (before AD 100), the Roman Tacitus (c. AD 120), the Roman Suetonius (c. AD 110), and the Roman governor Pliny the Younger (c. AD 110)—confirm many of the events, people, places, and customs chronicled in the New Testament. Early church leaders such as Irenaeus, Tertullian, Julius Africanus, and Clement of Rome—all writing before AD 250—also shed light on New Testament historical accuracy. Unlike Dan Brown, even skeptical historians agree that the New Testament is a remarkable historical document.

Massive Archaeological Evidence

As with the manuscript evidence, archaeology is a powerful witness to the accuracy of biblical documents. Over and over again, comprehensive archaeological fieldwork combined with careful biblical interpretation affirms the reliability of the Bible. It is telling when secular scholars must revise their biblical criticism in light of solid archaeological evidence.

For years, critics dismissed the book of Daniel, partly because there was no evidence that a king named Belshazzar ruled in Babylon during that period. Later archaeological research, however, confirmed that the reigning monarch, Nabonidus, appointed Belshazzar as his coregent while he was waging war away from Babylon.

One of the most well-known New Testament

examples concerns the books of Luke and Acts. Sir William Ramsay, a biblical skeptic who was trained as an archaeologist, set out to disprove the historical reliability of this portion of the New Testament. But through his painstaking archaeological trips throughout the Mediterranean region, he became converted as, one after another, the historical allusions of Luke were proved accurate.[3]

Furthermore, archaeologists recently discovered a gold mine of archaeological nuggets that provide a powerful counter to objections raised by some scholars against the biblical account of Christ's crucifixion and burial. In *U. S. News and World Report*, Jeffery Sheler highlights the significance of the discovery of the remains of a man crucified during the first century. This discovery calls into question the scholarship of liberals who contend that Jesus was tied rather than nailed to the cross and that his corpse was likely thrown into a shallow grave and eaten by wild dogs rather than entombed and resurrected.[4]

Finally, recent archaeological finds have also corroborated biblical details surrounding the trial that led to the fatal torment of Jesus Christ—including the existance of Pontius Pilate, the Roman governor of Judea who ordered Christ's crucifixion, and the burial site of Caiaphas, the high priest who presided over the religious trials of Christ. Sheler notes that in 1990 a burial chamber dating back to the first century was discovered two miles south of the Temple Mount. "Inside, archaeologists found 12 limestone ossuaries. One contained the bones of a 60-year-old man and bore the inscription *Yehosef bar Qayafa*—'Joseph, son of Caiaphas.' Experts believe these remains are almost certainly those of Caiaphas the high priest of Jerusalem, who according to the Gospels ordered the arrest of Jesus, interrogated him, and handed him over to Pontius Pilate for execution."[5]

Regarding Pontius Pilate, excavations at the seaside ruins of Caesarea Maritima—the ancient seat of the Roman government in Judea—uncovered a first-century inscription confirming that Pilate was the Roman ruler at the time of Christ's crucifixion.[6] Archeologists working at the Herodian theater found a plaque inscribed with the Latin words *Tiberieum . . . [Pon]tius Pilatus . . . [praef]ectus Juda[ea]e*. "According to experts, the complete inscription would have read, 'Pontius Pilate, the Prefect of Judea, has dedicated to the people of Caesarea a temple in honor of Tiberius.' The discovery of the so-called Pilate Stone has been widely acclaimed as a significant affirmation of biblical history because, in short, it confirms that the man depicted in the Gospels as Judea's Roman governor had precisely the responsibilities and authority that the Gospel writers ascribe to him."[7]

Truly, with every turn of the archaeologist's spade, we continue to see evidence for the trustworthiness of Scripture.

Messianic Prophecies

The Bible records predictions of events that could not have been known or predicted by chance or common sense. Surprisingly, the predictive nature of many Bible passages was once a popular argument (by liberals) *against* the reliability of the Bible. Critics argued that various passages must have been written later than the biblical texts indicated because they recounted events that occurred sometimes hundreds of years later than when the accounts were supposed to have been written. They concluded that, subsequent to the events, literary editors went back and doctored the original texts.

But such arguments are simply wrong. Careful research *affirms* the predictive accuracy of the Scriptures. For example, the previously mentioned book of Daniel (written before 530 BC)[8] accurately predicts the progression of kingdoms from Babylon through the Medo-Persian Empire, culminating in the persecution and suffering of the Jews under Antiochus IV Epiphanes, his desecration of the Jerusalem Temple, his untimely death, and freedom for the Jews under Judas Maccabeus in 165 BC.[9]

Old Testament prophecies concerning the Phoenician city of Tyre were fulfilled in ancient times, including prophecies that the city would be opposed by many nations (Ezekiel 26:3); its walls would be destroyed and towers broken down (26:4); and its stones, timbers, and debris would be thrown into the water (26:12). Similar prophecies were fulfilled concerning Sidon (Ezekiel 28:23; Isaiah 23; Jeremiah 27:3-6; 47:4) and Babylon (Jeremiah 50:13, 39; 51:26, 42-43, 58; Isaiah 13:20-21).

Since Christ is the Living Word of the New Testament and since his coming as Messiah is the culminating theme of the Old Testament, it should not surprise us that prophecies regarding him outnumber all others. Many of these prophecies would have been impossible for Jesus deliberately to conspire to fulfill—such as his descent from Abraham, Isaac, and Jacob (Genesis 12:3; 17:19; Matthew 1:1-2; Acts 3:25); his birth in Bethlehem (Micah 5:2; Matthew 2:1, 6); his crucifixion with criminals (Isaiah 53:12; Matthew 27:38); the piercing of his hands and feet on the cross (Psalm 22:16; John 20:25); the soldiers gambling for his clothes (Psalm 22:18; Matthew 27:35); the piercing of his side (Zechariah 12:10; John 19:34); the fact that his bones were not broken at his death (Psalm 34:20;

John 19:33-37); and his burial among the rich (Isaiah 53:9; Matthew 27:57-60).

Moreover, Jesus himself made predictions about the future, many of which stipulated fulfillment within the lifetimes of those who heard him prophesy. For example, Jesus predicted his own death and resurrection (John 2:19-22). Jesus also predicted the destruction of Jerusalem and the Jewish Temple (Luke 21)—a prophecy fulfilled to the minutest detail by the Roman general Titus in AD 70. The messianic prophesies fulfilled in Christ's life, death, and resurrection, as well as Jesus' own predictions, provide an empirically verifiable means of establishing the truth of his claims.

It is statistically preposterous to suppose that any or all of the Bible's specific, detailed prophecies could have been fulfilled through chance, good guessing, or deliberate deceit. When you consider some of the improbable prophecies cited above, it seems incredible that skeptics—knowing the authenticity and historicity of the texts—could reject the statistical verdict: the Bible is the Word of God.

DEMIGOD OR DEITY?

"My dear," Teabing declared, "until that moment in history, Jesus was viewed by His followers as a mortal

prophet . . . a great and powerful man,
but a *man* nonetheless. A mortal."
—*The Da Vinci Code*, PAGE 233 *(emphasis in original)*

Having demonstrated the utter falsity of Brown's claim that the Bible "evolved through countless translations, additions, and revisions" (231), we now turn to *The Da Vinci Code*'s blasphemous assertion that Jesus was merely a mortal man. According to the novel, Jesus was not regarded as divine until the fourth century, when the Council of Nicea turned him into a deity by "a relatively close vote." In reality, long before Nicea, the Bible chronicled Jesus as fully God. Not only so, but Jesus himself repeatedly claimed to be God and manifested the truth of his claim through the immutable fact of his resurrection.

The Bible Claims Jesus Is God

Since we have established that the Bible is not merely human but divine in origin, we can rightly appeal to Scripture to validate the deity of Christ. Three New Testament passages stand out as evidence in this regard. Not only are they clear and convincing, but their "addresses" are easy to remember as well—John 1, Colossians 1, and Hebrews 1.

First, we read in John 1:1, "In the beginning was the Word, and the Word was with God, and the Word was God." Here Jesus, referred to as "the Word" (Greek, *logos*), is not only in existence before the world began but is differentiated from the Father and explicitly called God, indicating that he shares the same nature as his Father.

Furthermore, Colossians 1 informs us that "all things were created by him" (verse 16); he is "before all things" (verse 17); and "God was pleased to have all his fullness dwell in him" (verse 19). Only deity has the prerogative of creation, preexists all things, and personifies the full essence and nature of God.

Finally, Hebrews 1 overtly tells us that Jesus is God—according to God the Father himself: "But about the Son he [the Father] says, 'Your throne, O God, will last for ever and ever'" (verse 8). Not only is the entirety of Hebrews 1 devoted to demonstrating the deity of Jesus, but in verses 10-12 the inspired writer quotes a passage from Psalms referring to Yahweh and directly applies it to Christ. In doing so, he unmistakably declares Jesus ontologically equal with Israel's God.

Many similar texts could be provided as additional evidence. For example, in Revelation 1 the Lord God says, "I am the Alpha and the Omega, who is, and who was, and who is to come, the Almighty" (verse 8). Then, in the last chapter of Revelation, Jesus applies these same words to himself! Additionally, in 2 Peter 1 Jesus is referred to as "our God and Savior Jesus Christ." In these passages and a host of others, the Bible explicitly claims that Jesus *is* God.

Jesus Claimed to Be God

When Jesus came to Caesarea Philippi, he asked his disciples the mother of all questions: *Who do you say that I am?* Dan Brown's response is, "You are 'a great and powerful man, but a *man* nonetheless. A mortal.'" (233). In sharp contrast, Simon Peter answered, "You are the Christ, the Son of the living God." Far from charging Peter with blasphemy, "Jesus replied, 'Blessed are you, Simon son of Jonah, for this was not revealed to you by man, but by my Father in heaven' " (Matthew 16:16-17). Like Peter, Jesus answered this all-important question by claiming to be God.

First, Jesus claimed to be the unique Son of God. As a result, the Jewish leaders tried to kill him because in "calling God his own Father, [Jesus was] making himself equal with God" (John 5:18). In John 8:58 Jesus went so far as to use the very words by which God revealed himself to Moses from the burning bush (Exodus 3:14). To the Jews this was the epitome of blasphemy, for they understood that Jesus was clearly claiming to be God. On yet another occasion, Jesus explicitly told the Jews: "'I and the Father are one.' Again the Jews picked up stones to stone him, but Jesus said to them, 'I have shown you many great miracles from the Father. For which of these do you stone me?' 'We are not stoning you for any of these,' replied the Jews, 'but for blasphemy, because you, a mere man, claim to be God'" (John 10:30-33).

Furthermore, Jesus made an unmistakable claim to deity before the chief priests and the whole Sanhedrin, the Jewish governing council. Caiaphas, the High Priest, asked him: "'Are you the Christ, the Son of the Blessed One?' 'I am,' said Jesus. 'And you will see the Son of Man sitting at the right hand of the Mighty One and coming on the clouds of heaven'" (Mark 14:61-62). A biblically illiterate person might well miss the import of Jesus' words, but Caiaphas and the council did not. They knew that in saying he was the *Son of Man* who would come *on the clouds of heaven*, Jesus was making an overt reference to the Son of Man in Daniel's prophecy (Daniel 7:13-14). He was not only claiming to be the preexistent Sovereign of the Universe but also prophesying that he would vindicate his claim by judging the very court that was now condemning him. Moreover, by combining Daniel's prophecy with David's proclamation in Psalm 110, Jesus was claiming that he would sit upon the throne of Israel's God and share God's very glory. To students of the Old Testament, this was the height of blasphemy; thus "they all condemned him as worthy of death" (Mark 14:64).

Finally, Jesus demonstrated that he possessed the very attributes of God. For example, he demonstrated *omniscience* by telling Peter, "this very night, before the rooster crows, you will disown me three times" (Matthew 26:34); declared *omnipotence* not only by resurrecting Lazarus (John 11:43) but by raising himself from the dead (see John 2:19); and professed *omnipresence* by promising he would be with his disciples "to the very end of the age" (Matthew 28:20). Not only so, but Jesus said to the paralytic in Luke 5:20, "Friend, your sins are forgiven." With these words he claimed a prerogative reserved for God alone. In addition, when Thomas worshiped Jesus saying, "My Lord and my God!" (John 20:28), Jesus responded with commendation rather than condemnation.

Christ's Credentials Substantiate His Claim to Deity

Jesus not only claimed to be God but also provided many convincing proofs that he indeed was divine. First, Jesus demonstrated that he was God in human flesh by manifesting the credential of sinlessness. While the Qur'an exhorts Muhammad to seek forgiveness for his sins, the Bible exonerates Messiah, saying Jesus "had no sin" (2 Corinthians 5:21). And this is not a singular statement. John declares, "in him is no sin" (1 John 3:5), and Peter says Jesus "committed no sin, and no deceit was found in his mouth" (1 Peter 2:22). Jesus himself went so far as to challenge his antagonists, asking, "Can any of you prove me guilty of sin?" (John 8:46).

Furthermore, Jesus demonstrated supernatural authority over sickness, the forces of nature, fallen angels, and even death itself. Matthew 4 records that Jesus went throughout Galilee teaching, preaching, and "healing every disease and sickness among the people" (verse 23). Mark 4 documents Jesus rebuking the wind and the waves, saying, "Quiet! Be still!" (verse 39). In Luke 4 Jesus encounters a man possessed by an evil spirit and commands the demon to "Come out of him!" (verse 35). And in John 4, Jesus tells a royal official whose son was close to death, "Your son will live" (verse 50). Jesus not only claimed to be the incarnate Son of God but also provided many convincing proofs that he was indeed divine, including fulfilling prophecy and performing miracles. And as we will see later, the most convincing proof of all is his resurrection from the dead.

Finally, the credentials of Christ's deity are seen in the lives of countless men, women, and children. Each day, people of every tongue and tribe and nation experience the resurrected Christ when they repent of their sins and receive Jesus as Lord and Savior of their lives. Thus, they not only come to know about Christ *evidentially*, but *experientially*. Christ becomes more real to his followers than the very flesh upon their bones.

MYSTERY RELIGIONS

> *Nothing* in Christianity is original. The pre-Christian God Mithras—called the Son of God and the Light of the World—was born on December 25, died, was buried in a rock tomb, and then resurrected in three days. By the way, December 25 is also the birthday of Osiris, Adonis, and Dionysus.
>
> —*The Da Vinci Code*, PAGE 232 *(emphasis in original)*

Having dispensed with *The Da Vinci Code*'s dogmatic assertions regarding the reliability of Scripture and deity of Christ, we now turn to Brown's contention that "Nothing in Christianity is original." Once again, however, what's not original are Brown's dogmatic assertions. He is simply repeating a common refrain sung by those who are determined to demean the biblical Jesus in the court of public opinion—namely that the death, burial, and resurrection of Jesus Christ are myths borrowed from ancient pagan mystery religions. This refrain, which once reverberated primarily through the bastions of private academia, is now all too common in the public arena.

The first prevailing myth widely circulated in this regard is that the similarities between Christianity and the mystery religions are striking.

Purveyors of this mythology employ biblical language and then go to great lengths to concoct commonalities. Take, for example, the alleged similarities between Christianity and the cult of Isis. The god Osiris was supposedly murdered by his brother and buried in the Nile. The goddess Isis recovered the cadaver, only to lose it once again to her brother-in-law, who cut the body into fourteen pieces and scattered them around the world. After finding the parts, Isis "baptized" each piece in the Nile River, and Osiris was "resurrected."

The alleged similarities as well as the terminology used to communicate them are greatly exaggerated. Parallels between the "resurrection" of Osiris and the resurrection of Christ are an obvious stretch.[10] Likewise, "The fate of Osiris's coffin in the Nile is as relevant to baptism as the sinking of Atlantis."[11] Sadly for the mysteries, this is as good as it gets. As philosopher Ronald Nash elaborates in his book *The Gospel and the Greeks*, other parallels cited by liberal scholars are even more far-fetched.[12] Not only that, but liberals have the chronology all wrong—most mysteries flourished long after the closing of the canon of Scripture. Thus, it would be far more accurate to say that the mysteries were influenced by Christianity than the other way around.[13]

Furthermore, the mystery religions reduced reality to a personal experience of enlightenment.

Through secret ceremonies initiates experienced an esoteric transformation of consciousness that led them to believe that they were entering a higher realm of reality. While followers of Christ were committed to essential Christian doctrines, devotees of the mysteries worked themselves into altered states of consciousness. They were committed to the notion that experience is a better teacher than words. In fact, the reason mystery religions are so named is that they involved secret practices and rites supposedly known only to the initiated. Far from being rooted in history and evidence, the mysteries reveled in hype and emotionalism.

Finally, the mystery religions as a rule fused together various forms of multiple religious systems. Adherents not only worshiped a variety of pagan deities but also frequently embraced aspects of competing mystery religions while continuing to worship within their own cultic constructs. Not so with Christianity. Followers of Christ singularly placed their faith in the One who said, "I am the way and the truth and the life. No one comes to the Father except through me" (John 14:6).

RESURRECTION—THE ULTIMATE VINDICATION

If *The Da Vinci Code* is correct, the resurrection of Christ is mere mythology borrowed from the pagan cult of Mithras. If, on the other hand, the biblical account of the Resurrection is true, it provides the ultimate vindication of Christianity. No middle ground exists. The Resurrection is either history or hoax, miracle or myth, fact or fantasy. If the Resurrection never happened, then Christianity has no basis. Thus, before we bring this book to a close it is crucial to examine the historicity of the Resurrection.

The first convincing piece of evidence for the Resurrection is the empty tomb. Liberal and conservative scholars alike agree that the body of Jesus was buried in the private tomb of Joseph of Arimathea, a member of the Jewish court that condemned Jesus (Mark 15:43).[14] Jesus' burial in Joseph's tomb is substantiated by Mark's Gospel (15:46) and is, therefore, far too early to have been the subject of legendary corruption. The earliest Jewish response to the resurrection of Christ presupposes the empty tomb (Matthew 28:11-13). In the centuries since the Resurrection, the fact of the empty tomb has been accepted by Jesus' friends and foes alike.[15] In short, the absence of a tomb containing the identifiable corpse of Christ argues for the reliability of the Resurrection. Additionally, when you understand that women in first-century Jewish society were viewed as having a status far less than that of men, it is extraordinary that the account would feature females as the discoverers of the empty tomb. The fact that the Gospels record women as the first witnesses to the empty tomb is most plausibly explained by the reality that—like it or not—they *were* the discoverers of the empty tomb. This shows that the Gospel writers faithfully recorded what happened, even if it was embarrassing according to the cultural customs of the time.

Furthermore, Jesus gave his disciples many convincing proofs that he had risen from the dead. For example, Paul points out that Christ "appeared to more than five hundred of the brothers at the same time, most of whom are still living, though some have fallen asleep" (1 Corinthians 15:6).[16] It would have been one thing to attribute these supernatural experiences to people who had already died. It was quite another to attribute them to multitudes who were still alive. As famed New Testament scholar C. H. Dodd points out, "There can hardly be any purpose in mentioning the fact that most of the five hundred are still alive, unless Paul is saying in effect, 'The witnesses are there to be questioned.'"

Finally, what happened as a result of the Resurrection is unprecedented in human history. In the span of a few hundred years, a small band of seemingly insignificant believers succeeded in turning an entire empire upside down. While it is conceivable that they would have faced torture, vilification, and even cruel deaths for what they fervently believed to be true, it is inconceivable that they would have been willing to die for what they knew to be a lie. As Dr. Simon Greenleaf, the famous Royall Professor of Law at Harvard, put it: "If it were morally possible for them to have been deceived in this matter, every human motive operated to lead them to discover and avow their error. . . . If then their testimony was not true, there was no possible motive for this fabrication."

The Twelve

As Greenleaf so masterfully communicates, the Twelve[17] were thoroughly transformed by the Resurrection.

Peter, who was once so afraid of being exposed as a follower of Christ that he denied he even knew Jesus, after the Resurrection was transformed into a lion of the faith. According to tradition, he was crucified upside down because he felt unworthy to be crucified in the same manner as his Lord.[18]

James, the brother of Jesus, who once hated everything his brother stood for, after the Resurrection called himself a bondservant of Jesus Christ.[19] He not only became the leader of the Jerusalem church but was martyred for his faith. Eusebius of Caesarea describes how James was thrown from the pinnacle of the Temple and subsequently stoned.[20]

Paul, likewise, was transformed. Once a ceaseless persecutor of the growing church, he became the chief proselytizer of the Gentiles. His radical transformation is underscored by his testimony in his letter to the Philippians:

> But whatever was to my profit I now consider loss for the sake of Christ. What is more, I consider everything a loss compared to the surpassing greatness of knowing Christ Jesus my Lord, for whose sake I have lost all things. I consider them rubbish, that I may gain Christ and be found in him, not having a righteousness of my own that comes from the law, but that which is through faith in Christ—the righteousness that comes from God and is by faith. I want to know Christ and the power of his resurrection and the fellowship of sharing in his sufferings, becoming like him in his death, and so, somehow, to attain to the resurrection from the dead. *(Philippians 3:7-11)*

Peter, James, and Paul were not alone. As Christian philosopher J. P. Moreland points out, within weeks of the Resurrection not just one but an entire community of at least ten thousand Jews were willing to give up the very sociological and theological traditions that had given them their national identity.[21]

Traditions

Among the traditions that were transformed after the Resurrection were the Sabbath, the sacrifices, and the sacraments.

In Genesis the Sabbath was a celebration of God's work in creation.[22] After the Exodus, the Sabbath expanded to a celebration of God's deliverance from the oppression of Egypt.[23] As a result of the Resurrection, the Sabbath shifted once again. It became a celebration of the "rest" we have through Christ who delivers us from sin and the grave.[24] In remembrance of the Resurrection, the early Christian church changed the day of worship from the Sabbath (Saturday) to Sunday. God himself provided the early church with a new pattern of worship through Christ's resurrection on the first day of the week, his subsequent Sunday appearances, and the Spirit's Sunday descent.[25] For the emerging Christian church, the most dangerous snare was a failure to recognize that Jesus was the substance that fulfilled the symbol of the Sabbath.

For Jewish believers the sacrificial system was radically transformed by the resurrection of Christ as well. The Jews had been taught from the time of Abraham that they were to sacrifice animals as the symbol of atonement for sin. However, after the Resurrection the followers of Christ suddenly stopped sacrificing. They recognized that the new covenant was better than the old covenant because the blood of Jesus Christ was better than the blood of animals.[26] They finally understood that Jesus was the substance that fulfilled the symbol. He was the sacrificial lamb that takes away the sin of the world.[27]

Like the Sabbath and the sacrificial system, the Jewish rites of Passover and baptism were radically transformed. In place of the Passover meal, believers celebrated the Lord's Supper. Moreland points out that Jesus had just been slaughtered in grotesque and humiliating fashion, yet the disciples remembered the broken body and shed blood of Christ with joy. Only the Resurrection can account for that! Imagine devotees of John F. Kennedy getting together to celebrate his murder at the hands of Lee Harvey Oswald. They may well celebrate his confrontations with communism, his contributions to civil rights, or his captivating charisma, but never his brutal killing.[28]

In like fashion baptism was radically transformed. Gentile converts to Judaism were baptized in the name of the God of Israel.[29] After the Resurrection, converts to Christianity were baptized in the name of Jesus Christ.[30] Thus, Christ was shown to have the very status of God.[31] Only the Resurrection could account for that.

SO, WHAT ABOUT YOU?

At this point you have had the opportunity to examine the historical authenticity of the claims made in *The Da Vinci Code.* In addition, you have encountered a positive defense of the faith—namely, that the Bible is divine rather than human in origin, that Jesus Christ is God in human flesh, and that amid the religions of the ancient world, Christianity is demonstrably unique. But there is more. Christianity is not merely objectively true; Christianity can be subjectively experienced as well. So, what about you?

If you are already a believer, you have experienced the peace and joy that only Jesus Christ can bring to the human heart. If you are not, we want to give you that opportunity right now. In essence, it involves realizing that you are a sinner, being willing to repent of your sins, and then receiving Jesus Christ as the Savior and Lord of your life.

REALIZE THAT YOU ARE A SINNER

Sin is not just murder, rape, or robbery. Sin is failing to do the things you should and doing those things you should not. In short, *sin* is a word that describes anything that fails to meet God's standard of perfection. As such, sin is the barrier between you and a satisfying relationship with God. As Scripture puts it, "Your iniquities [sins] have separated you from your God" (Isaiah 59:2).

Just as light and dark cannot exist together, neither can God and sin. Each day we are further separated from God as we add to the account of our sin. But that is not the only problem. Sin also separates us from others. You need only read the newspaper or listen to a news report to see how true this really is. Locally, we read of murder, robbery, and fraud. Nationally, we hear of corruption in politics, racial tension, and an escalating rate of suicide. Internationally, we see a constant succession of wars. We live in a time when terrorism abounds and when the world as we know it can be instantly obliterated by nuclear aggression.

All of these things are indicative of sin. The Bible says that we "all have sinned and fall short of the glory of God" (Romans 3:23). The question is whether or not you are willing to repent of your sin.

REPENT OF YOUR SIN

Repentance is an old English word that describes a willingness to turn from sin toward Jesus Christ. It literally means a complete U-turn on the road of life—a change of heart and a change of mind. It means a willingness to follow Jesus Christ and receive him as Savior and Lord. In the words of Christ, "The time has come. . . . The kingdom of God is near. Repent and believe the good news!" (Mark 1:15).

RECEIVE JESUS CHRIST AS SAVIOR AND LORD

To demonstrate true belief means to be willing to receive God's free gift. To truly receive God's gift is to trust in and depend on Jesus Christ alone to be the Lord of your life here and now and your Savior for all eternity.

Receiving God's free gift takes more than knowledge. It takes more than agreeing that the knowledge is accurate. True saving faith entails not only knowledge and agreement, but trust. By way of illustration, when you are sick you can know that a particular medicine can cure you. You can even agree that it has cured thousands of others. But until you trust it enough to take it, it cannot cure *you*. In like manner, you can know about Jesus Christ, and you can agree that he has saved others, but until you personally place your trust in him, you will not be saved. The requirements for eternal life are not based on what *you can do* but on what *Jesus Christ has done*. He stands ready to exchange his perfection for your imperfection.

To those who have never received him as Savior and Lord, Jesus says, "Here I am! I stand at the door and knock. If anyone hears my voice and opens the door, I will come in" (Revelation 3:20). Jesus knocks on the door of the human heart, and the question he asks is, Are you ready *now* to receive me as your Savior and Lord?

APPLICATION

Even now, if the Spirit of God is moving upon your heart, you can receive the resurrected Christ as your personal Savior and Lord. To do so, simply pray this prayer—and remember, there is no magic in the words, God is looking at the intent of your heart.

> *Heavenly Father,*
> *I thank you that you have provided a way for me to have a relationship with you;*
> *I realize that I am a sinner;*
> *I thank you that you are my perfect Father;*
> *I thank you for sending Jesus to be my Savior and Lord;*
> *I repent and receive his perfection in exchange for my sin.*
> *Amen.*

The assurance of eternal life is found in these words from Jesus Christ: "I tell you the truth, whoever hears my word and believes him who sent me has eternal life and will not be condemned; he has crossed over from death to life" (John 5:24).

Based on God's promise, you now have eternal life—you have crossed over from death to life! With new life must come growth. Each day we have the opportunity to grow in our relationship with God. Each day this relationship can become more precious and meaningful. We'd like to conclude by giving you three basic steps that will help you grow as a disciple of Jesus Christ.

First, no relationship can flourish without constant, heartfelt communication. This is true not only in human relationships, but also in our relationship with God. If you are to nurture a strong walk with our Savior, you must be in constant communication with him. The way to do that is through prayer. The more time you spend with God in prayer, the more intimate your relationship will be.

Furthermore, it is crucial that as a new believer you spend time reading God's written revelation of himself—the Bible. The Bible not only forms the foundation of an effective prayer life, it is foundational to every other aspect of Christian living. While prayer is our primary way of communicating with God, the Bible is God's primary way of communicating with us. Nothing should take precedence over getting into the Word and getting the Word into us. I generally recommend that new believers begin by reading one chapter from the Gospel of John each day. As you do, you will experience the joy of having God speak to you through his Word. As Jesus put it, "I am the bread of life. He who comes to me will never go hungry, and he who believes in me will never be thirsty" (John 6:35).

Finally, it is crucial to become an active participant in a healthy, well-balanced church. In Scripture, the church is referred to as the body of Christ. Just as our body is one and yet has many parts, so the body of Christ is one but is composed of many members. Those who receive Christ as the Savior and Lord of their lives are already a part of the church universal. It is crucial, however, that all Christians become vital, reproducing members of a local body of believers as well. It is in the local church where God is worshiped through prayer, praise, and proclamation; where believers experience fellowship with one another; and where they are equipped to reach others through the testimony of their love, their lips, and their lives.

NOTES

FOREWORD

1 Leon Wieseltier, "The Worship of Blood: Mel Gibson's Lethal Weapon," *New Republic*, February 26, 2004, http://www.tnr.com/.

2 Maureen Dowd, "Stations of the Crass," *New York Times*, February 26, 2004, http://www.nytimes.com/.

3 Andy Rooney, *60 Minutes* (CBS), aired February 22, 2004.

4 Dan Brown, *The Da Vinci Code* (New York: Doubleday, 2003).

5 Jeff Ayers, *Library Journal*, (February 1, 2003): 114.

6 *Publisher's Weekly*, (March 18, 2003): 76.

7 Brown, *The Da Vinci Code*, back cover.

8 Dan Brown, interview by Charles Gibson, *Good Morning America*, ABC, November 3, 2003. The following exchange between Charles Gibson and Dan Brown occurred on *Good Morning America*, ABC, November 3, 2003. CHARLES GIBSON: ". . . This is a novel. If you were writing it as a non-fiction book. . . . how would it have been different?" DAN BROWN: "I don't think it would have. I began the research for 'The Da Vinci Code' as a skeptic. I entirely expected, as I researched the book, to disprove this theory. And after numerous trips to Europe, about two years of research, I really became a believer. And it's important to remember that this is a novel about a theory that has been out there for a long time" (ABC News Transcripts). Additionally, on *Primetime Live (Monday): Jesus, Mary and Da Vinci*, ABC, which aired November 3, 2003, Brown told Elizabeth Vargas, "I began as a skeptic. As I started researching 'Da Vinci Code,' I really thought I would disprove a lot of this theory about Mary Magdalene and holy blood and all of that. I became a believer" (ABC News Transcripts).

PART ONE
THE DA VINCI DECEPTION

1 Consider, for example, the *fatwa* decreeing death for Salmon Rushdie because of his book *The Satanic Verses*.

2 Hugh J. Schonfield, *The Passover Plot—A New Interpretation of the Life and Death of Jesus* (London: Harper Collins reprint, 1998).

3 Nikos Kazantzakis, *The Last Temptation of Christ* (New York: Simon & Schuster, 1960).

4 S. G. F. Brandon, *Jesus and the Zealots: A Study of the Political Factor in Primitive Christianity* (New York: Charles Scribner, 1967). See also, by the same author, *The Trial of Jesus of Nazareth* (New York: Stein & Day, 1955).

5 John M. Allegro, *The Sacred Mushroom and the Cross* (Garden City: Doubleday, 1970).

6 Morton Smith, *The Secret Gospel: The Discovery and Interpretation of the Secret Gospel According to Mark* (New York: Harper & Row, 1973). See also, by the same author, *Jesus the Magician: Charlatan or Son of God?* (New York: Harper & Row, 1978).

7 Donovan Joyce, *The Jesus Scroll* (New York: Signet, 1974).

8 Michael Baigent, Richard Leigh, and Henry Lincoln, *Holy Blood, Holy Grail* (New York: reprint by Delacorte Press, 2004). Several earlier books had presented the married Jesus hypothesis, including William E. Phipps, *Was Jesus Married?* (New York: Harper & Row, 1970).

9 John Dominic Crossan, *The Historical Jesus: The Life of a Mediterranean Jewish Peasant.* (HarperSanFrancisco, 1993). There are very few episodes in the traditional life of Jesus that Crossan has not managed to challenge with the most arbitrary conclusions.

10 Dan Brown, *The Da Vinci Code* (New York: Doubleday, 2003).

11 *New York Times* best-selling author, Nelson DeMille.

12 Taylor Caldwell, *Great Lion of God* (Garden City: Doubleday, 1970). The same author showed her exuberant imagination in a similar novel about St. Luke, *Dear and Glorious Physician.*

13 Dan Brown, interview by Charles Gibson, *Good Morning America*, ABC, November 3, 2003, and *Primetime Live (Monday): Jesus, Mary and Da Vinci*, ABC, November 3, 2003. See additional information in endnote 8 in the Foreword. See also Renee Tawa, "Deep into the 'Code,'" *Los Angeles Times* (Friday, March 19, 2004).

14 In a brilliant article in the *New York Times*, Laura Miller exposes the entire hoax. See Laura Miller, "The Da Vinci Con," *The New York Times Book Review* (Sunday, February 22, 2004), 23.

15 Eusebius of Caesarea, the Christian historian who detailed the first three centuries of Christianity, provides abundant

evidence that the canon was well established before the time of Constantine. See Eusebius, *Church History*, 3.3-4, 24-25; 5.8; 6.14, 25. If Constantine *had* had any role whatever in collating or deciding on the canon, Eusebius would have been the first to report that, since he greatly admired the first Christian emperor.

16 In the 19th century, the Swiss historian, Jacob Burckhardt—like Dan Brown—disputed Constantine's conversion, claiming that his actions in behalf of Christianity were done on the basis of cold political calculation rather than conscientious conviction, a strategy to use the church for partisan political support. The great majority of modern historians, however, conclude that Constantine's conversion was indeed genuine, since the evidence is overwhelming. A whole array of book titles and scholarly articles deal with the life of Constantine, and most would agree with the masterful study by Timothy D. Barnes, who states: "With all his faults . . . [Constantine] nevertheless believed sincerely that God had given him a special mission to convert the Roman Empire to Christianity." Timothy D. Barnes, *Constantine and Eusebius* (Cambridge, MA: Harvard University Press, 1981), 275. See also Paul L. Maier, *Eusebius–The Church History* (Grand Rapids: Kregel, 1999), 306ff.

17 Sunday is called "the Lord's Day" in Ignatius, Justin Martyr, and later, in *Didache* 14, as well as in a treatise by Melito of Sardis (died c. 190) called *The Lord's Day*. Of these references, that of Pliny the Younger—as a pagan—is the most interesting. In his letter to the emperor Trajan (AD 117–138) regarding Christians in Asia Minor, Pliny writes that the Christians "met regularly before dawn on a fixed day to chant verses alternately amongst themselves in honor of Christ as if to a god." (Betty Radice, ed., *The Letters of Pliny the Younger* [Baltimore: Penguin Books, 1967] 294.) In Acts 20:7, when St. Paul visited the Christians at Troas "on the first day of the week," that day began (in Jewish fashion) on Saturday evening when they were accustomed to "break bread," i.e., the Lord's Supper. Under Trajan, since these evening gatherings were prohibited, the "fixed day" to which Pliny refers was moved to before dawn on Sunday.

18 The two dissenting bishops were Secundus of Ptolemais and Theonas of Marmarica, both Libyan bishops associated with Arius. All three went into exile after the Council of Nicea. See Timothy D. Barnes, *Constantine and Eusebius*, 217.

19 For the origin of the Knights Templar, the most important primary source is the chronicler William of Tyre, *Historia rerum in partibus transmarinis gestarum*, xii, 7. Most of the secondary literature is in French, while the classic in English is: G. G. Addison, *The History of the Knights Templars, the Temple Church, and the*

Temple 3rd ed., 1852; New York: AMS Press reprint, 1978. See also G. A. Campbell, *The Knights Templar* (New York: AMS Press, 1980); Helen Nicholson, *The Knights Templar: A New History* (Stroud, UK: Sutton, 2001); and Frank Sanello, *The Knights Templar: God's Warriors and the Devil's Bankers* (Lanham, MD: Taylor, 2003).

20 For true, rather than contrived, historical detail regarding Leonardo da Vinci, see V. P. Zubov, *Leonardo da Vinci* (Cambridge: Harvard University Press, 1968); Patrice Boussel, *Leonardo da Vinci* (Secaucus, NJ: Chartwell, 1980); Kenneth Clark, *Leonardo da Vinci* (New York: Viking, 1988); and Sherwin B. Nuland, *Leonardo da Vinci* (New York: Viking, 2000).

For a good supplementary critique of *The Da Vinci Code*, please see Sandra Miesel, "Dismantling The Da Vinci Code," http://www.crisismagazine.com/September2003/feature1.htm.

21 For the Olympic Games, see M. I. Finley and H.W. Pleket, *The Olympic Games: The First Thousand Years* (New York: Viking, 1976); J. Kieran and A. Dailey, *The Story of the Olympic Games* (Philadelphia: Lippincott, 1977); B. Henry and R. Yeoman, *An Approved History of the Olympic Games* (Sherman Oaks, CA: Alfred, 1984); and Allen Guttmann, *The Olympics: A History of the Modern Games* (Urbana, IL: University of Illinois Press, 1992).

22 See previous Eusebius references at note 15.

23 The early core of Paris was on the Île de la Cité. a natural stronghold already in the third century BC, which was owned by the tribe of the Parisi. The Romans conquered and called the place Lutetia, but the name changed to Paris between AD 305 and 310. Clovis, founder of the Merovingian dynasty, moved his capital to Paris about AD 500.

24 The best primary source for this information is Eddius Stephanus, *Vita Wilfridi.* See Bertram Colgrave, *The Life of Bishop Wilfrid* (1927; repr., New York: Cambridge University Press, 1985), 66–69. I am indebted to Western Michigan University's distinguished Medievalist, Professor Tom Amos, for the specifics regarding Dagobert.

25 For a good supplementary critique of *The Da Vinci Code*, please see Sandra Miesel, "Dismantling The Da Vinci Code," http://www.crisismagazine.com/September2003/feature1.htm.

PART TWO
BUT WHAT IS TRUTH?

1 The New Testament was originally written in Greek. Nearly all of the Greek manuscripts that exist today predate the invention of the printing press, and some 800 predate AD 1000. Lee

Strobel, interviewing Dr. Bruce Metzger of Princeton Theological Seminary, provides an excellent summary of the various types of manuscripts:

> While *papyrus* manuscripts represent the earliest copies of the New Testament, there are also ancient copies written on *parchment*, which was made from the skins of cattle, sheep, goats and antelope.
>
> We have what are called *uncial* manuscripts, which are written in all-capital Greek letters,' Metzger explained. 'Today we have 306 of these, several dating back as early as the third century. The most important are *Codex Sinaiticus*, which is the only complete New Testament in uncial letters, and *Codex Vaticanus*, which is not quite complete. Both date to about AD 350.
>
> A new style of writing, more cursive in nature, emerged in roughly AD 800. It's called *minuscule*, and we have 2,856 of these manuscripts. Then there are also *lectionaries*, which contain New Testament Scripture in the sequence it was to be read in the early churches at appropriate times during the year. A total of 2,403 of these have been cataloged. That puts the grand total of Greek manuscripts at 5,664. (Lee Strobel, *The Case for Christ* [Grand Rapids: Zondervan, 1998], 62–63.)

The acronym L-U-M-P can be used as a memory aid so as not to *lump* all the varieties of manuscripts together—*L*exionaries, *U*ncials, *M*iniscules, and *P*apyri.

2 The earliest New Testament manuscript fragments date to the first and second centuries AD, within 30 to 50 years of the original writing. More than 40 remaining Greek manuscripts date *before* the fourth century—several from the second century—collectively composing most of the New Testament. The earliest existing copy of an entire New Testament text is *Codex Sinaiticus* (c. 350); *Codex Vaticanus* (c. 325) also contains the entire New Testament except Pastoral Epistles and Revelation. Note also that virtually the entire New Testament can be reconstructed from quotations found in the writings of the early church fathers.

According to New Testament scholar Craig Blomberg, the standard dating of the Gospels (which is accepted even among very liberal scholars) sets "Mark in the 70s, Matthew and Luke in the 80s, and John in the 90s." If these dates are correct, Blomberg points out, they are well within the lifetimes of the "eyewitnesses of the life of Jesus, including hostile eyewitnesses who would have served as a corrective if false teachings about Jesus were going around" (Lee Strobel, *The Case for Christ* [Grand Rapids: Zondervan, 1998], 33). Of course, if the earliest manuscripts do indeed date to the first century, then the original writing of the New Testament would be pushed back even earlier, so we can all the more infer that the New Testament was written within the lifetimes of the community that bore witness to the events described therein.

See also Carsten Peter Thiede and Matthew d'Ancona, *Eyewitness to Jesus* (New York: Doubleday, 1996), 29–31, chap. 5; and Philip Wesley Comfort, ed. *The Origin of the Bible* (Wheaton: Tyndale House Publishers, 1992), 179–207.

3 See William M Ramsay, *The Bearing of Recent Discovery on the Trustworthiness of the New Testament*, reprint ed. (Grand Rapids, MI: Baker, 1953).

4 Sheler explains, "Explorers found the skeletal remains of a crucified man in a burial cave at Giva'at ha-Mitvar, near the Nablus road outside of Jerusalem. It was a momentous discovery: While the Romans were known to have crucified thousands of alleged traitors, rebels, robbers, and deserters in the two centuries straddling the turn of the era, never before had the remains of a crucifixion victim been recovered. An initial analysis of the remains found that their condition dramatically corroborated the Bible's description of the Roman method of execution.

"The bones were preserved in a stone burial box called an ossuary and appeared to be those of a man about 5 feet, 5 inches tall and 24 to 28 years old. His open arms had been nailed to the crossbar, in the manner similar to that shown in crucifixion paintings. The knees had been doubled up and turned sideways, and a single large iron nail had been driven through both heels. The nail—still lodged in the heel bone of one foot, though the executioners had removed the body from the cross after death—was found bent, apparently having hit a knot in the wood. The shin bones seem to have been broken, corroborating what the Gospel of John suggests was normal practice in Roman crucifixions." (Jeffrey L. Sheler, "Is the Bible True?" *U. S. News and World Report*, (October 25, 1999): 58; reprinted from Jeffrey L. Sheler, *Is the Bible True?* (San Francisco: HarperSanFrancisco, 1999).

5 Ibid., 58–59.

6 See Paul L. Maier, *In the Fullness of Time: A Historian Looks at Christmas, Easter, and the Early Church* (HarperSanFrancisco, 1991), 145ff.

7 Jeffrey L. Sheler, "Is the Bible True?" *U. S. News and World Report*, (October 25, 1999): 59. Sheler discusses other archaeological and historical insights of recent years as well, including the House of David inscription at Dan, which affirms the historicity of King David (54–58).

8 According to Old Testament scholar Gleason Archer, "Despite the numerous objections which have been advanced by scholars who regard this as a prophecy written after the event, there is no good reason for denying the sixth-century Daniel the composition of the entire work. This represents a collection of his memoirs made at the end of a long and eventful career which included government service from the reign of Nebuchadnezzar in the 590s to the reign of Cyrus the Great in the 530s. The appearance of Persian technical terms indicates a final recension of these memoirs at a time when Persian terminology had already infiltrated into the vocabulary of Aramaic. The most likely date for the final edition of the book, therefore, would be about 530 BC, nine years after the Persian conquest of Babylon." Gleason L. Archer, *A Survey of Old Testament Introduction*, rev. ed. (Chicago: Moody Press, 1994), 423; see 423–447 for discussion.

9 Chapters 2 and 7 of the Old Testament book of Daniel describe Daniel's prophesies related to the coming kingdoms; Daniel's vision in chapter 8 represents details of Antiochus Epiphanes' reign in the second century BC. The "horn" that "started small but grew in power . . . until it reached the host of the heavens" represents Antiochus Epiphanes.

10 Historian Edwin Yamauchi explains: "It is a cardinal misconception to equate the Egyptian view of the afterlife with the 'resurrection' of Hebrew-Christian traditions. In order to achieve immortality the Egyptian had to fulfill three conditions: (1) His body had to be preserved, hence mummification. (2) Nourishment had to be provided either by the actual offering of daily bread and beer, or by the magical depiction of food on the walls of the tomb. (3) Magical spells had to be interred with the dead-Pyramid Texts in the Old Kingdom, Coffin Texts in the Middle Kingdom, and the Book of the Dead in the New Kingdom. Moreover, the Egyptian did not rise from the dead; separate entities of his personality such as his Ba and his Ka continued to hover about his body. Nor is Osiris, who is always portrayed in a mummified form, an inspiration for the resurrected Christ. As Roland de Vaux has observed: 'What is meant of Osiris being "raised to life"? Simply that, thanks to the ministrations of Isis, he is able to lead a life beyond the tomb which is an almost perfect replica of earthly existence. But he will never again come among the living and will reign only over the dead. . . . This revived god is in reality a "mummy" god' [The Bible and the Ancient Near East, 1971, p. 236]." (Edwin M. Yamauchi, "Easter: Myth, Hallucination, or History?" *Christianity Today*, March 29, 1974, available at http://www.leaderu.com/everystudent/easter/articles/yama.html (accessed March 10, 2004). See also Ronald Nash, "Was the New Testament Influenced by Pagan

Religions?" *Christian Research Journal*, vol. 16 (no. 2), available at http://www.equip.org/ free/DB109.pdf, accessed 10 March 2004.)

11 Ronald Nash, "Was the New Testament Influenced by Pagan Religions?" *Christian Research Journal*, vol. 16 (no. 2), 11.

12 Ronald H. Nash, *The Gospel and the Greeks*, 2nd ed. (Phillipsburg, NJ: Presbyterian and Reformed, 2003). For an excellent summary overview, see Nash, "Was the New Testament Influenced by Pagan Religions?" available at http://www.equip.org/free/DB109.pdf.

13 See Nash, "Was the New Testament Influenced by Pagan Religions?"

14 The champion of the line of argumentation I follow is the philosopher and Christian apologist William Lane Craig. See especially his chapter "Did Jesus Rise from the Dead?" in Michael J. Wilkins and J. P. Moreland, eds., *Jesus Under Fire: Modern Scholarship Reinvents the Historical Jesus* (Grand Rapids: Zondervan, 1995), 141–176; his contribution throughout Paul Copan and Ronald K. Tacelli, eds., *Jesus' Resurection: Fact or Figment? A Debate between William Lane Craig and Gerd Lüdemann* (Downers Grove, IL: InterVarsity Press, 2000); and William Lane Craig, *Reasonable Faith*, revised edition (Wheaton, IL: Crossway Books, 1994), 255–298.

15 The late liberal scholar John A. T. Robinson of Cambridge conceded that the burial of Christ "is one of the earliest and best-attested facts about Jesus" (John A. T. Robinson, *The Human Face of God* [Philadelphia: Westminster, 1973], 131, as quoted in Paul Copan, ed., *Will the Real Jesus Please Stand Up? A Debate between William Lane Craig and John Dominic Crossan* (Grand Rapids: Baker Books, 1998), 27). Also, New Testament critic D. H. van Daalen has noted, "It is extremely difficult to object to the empty tomb on historical grounds; those who deny it do so on the basis of theological or philosophical assumptions" (as quoted in William Lane Craig, "Contemporary Scholarship and the Historical Evidence for the Resurrection of Jesus Christ," *Truth* 1 [1985]: 89–95, available at http://www.leaderu.com/truth/1truth22.html).

16 In 1 Corinthians 15:3-8 Paul is reiterating a Christian creed that can be traced all the way back to the formative stages of the early Christian church. Incredibly, New Testament scholars of all stripes agree that this creed can be dated to within three to eight years of the crucifixion itself. In his seminal work titled *The Historical Jesus: Ancient Evidence for the Life of Christ*, Dr. Gary Habermas lists a variety of reasons by which scholars have come to this conclusion. First, Paul employs technical Jewish terminology used to transmit oral tradition when he uses such words as "delivered" and "received." Scholars view this as evidence that

Paul is reciting information he received from another source. The eminent scholar Joachim Jeremias, a leading authority on this issue, also points to non-Pauline phrases such as 'for our sins' (verse 3); 'according to the Scriptures' (verses 3-4); 'he has been raised' (verse 4); the 'third day' (verse 4); 'he was seen' (verses 5-8); and 'the twelve' (verse 5). Furthermore, "the creed is organized in a stylized, parallel form" that reflects an oral tradition. Finally, Paul's use of the Aramaic word *Cephas* for Peter points to an extremely early Semitic source. (See Gary R. Habermas, *The Historical Jesus: Ancient Evidence for the Life of Christ* [Joplin, Missouri: College Press Publishing Co., 1996], 153-54.)

17 See 1 Corinthians 15:5, where the original apostles, minus Judas, are referred to as the Twelve.

18 See Eusebius, *History of the Church*, 2.25;3.1; Clement of Rome, *First Epistle to the Corinthians*, chap. 5.

19 James 1:1 (NASB).

20 Eusebius, *History of the Church* 2.23. Cf. Josephus, *Antiquities*, 20.9.1; see John P. Meier, *A Marginal Jew: Rethinking the Historical Jesus*, vol. 1 (New York: Doubleday, 1991), 57-9.

21 Lee Strobel, *The Case for Christ* (Grand Rapids: Zondervan, 1998), 251.

22 See Genesis 2:2-3; cf. Exodus 20:11.

23 See Deuteronomy 5:15.

24 See Colossians 2:17; Hebrews 4:1-11.

25 Norman Geisler and Thomas Howe, *When Critics Ask* (Wheaton: Victor Books, 1992), 78. See Matthew 28:1-10; John 20:26ff; Acts 2:1; 20:7; 1 Corinthians 16:2.

26 See Hebrews 8-10.

27 See John 1:29.

28 Adapted from Strobel, *The Case for Christ* (Grand Rapids: Zondervan, 1998), 253.

29 "Proselytes entering Judaism were expected to strip themselves of their former clothing, submit to circumcision, and bathe themselves completely, after which they were reckoned members of the Jewish community. The rite was acknowledgment of defilement and of the acceptance of the law as a purifying agent." (Carl F. H. Henry, ed., *Basic Christian Doctrines* [Grand Rapids: Baker Book House, 1971], 256.)

30 See Acts 2:36-41.

31 Adapted from Strobel, 253.

FOR FURTHER READING

HISTORICITY OF JESUS AND THE RESURRECTION

Gary R. Habermas, *The Historical Jesus: Ancient Evidence for the Life of Christ* (Joplin, MO: College Press Publishing Co., 1996).

Hank Hanegraaff, *The Third Day* (Nashville: W Publishing Group, 2003).

Paul L. Maier, *In the Fullness of Time: A Historian Looks at Christmas, Easter, and the Early Church* (HarperSanFrancisco, 1991; Grand Rapids: Kregel, 1997).

EVIDENCE FOR JESUS OUTSIDE THE NEW TESTAMENT

Gary R. Habermas, *The Historical Jesus: Ancient Evidence for the Life of Christ* (Joplin, MO: College Press Publishing Co., 1996).

Paul L. Maier, *Josephus: The Essential Works* (Grand Rapids: Kregel, 1988).

THE BIBLE AND THE EARLY CHURCH

F.F. Bruce, *The Canon of Scripture* Downers Grove, IL: InterVarsity Press, 1988).

Paul L. Maier, *Eusebius—The Church History* (Grand Rapids: Kregel, 1999).

THE NEW TESTAMENT AND PAGAN RELIGIONS

Ronald Nash, "Was the New Testament Influenced by Pagan Religions?" *Christian Research Journal*, vol. 16 (no. 2), available at www.equip.org/ free/DB109.pdf.

CHRISTIAN RESEARCH INSTITUTE

The Christian Research Institute (CRI) exists to provide Christians with carefully researched information and well-reasoned answers that encourage their faith and equip them to intelligently represent it to people influenced by ideas that undermine orthodox, biblical Christianity. In carrying out this mission, CRI's strategy is expressed by the acronym *E-Q-U-I-P*:

The *E* represents *essentials*. CRI is committed to the maxim "In essentials unity, in nonessentials liberty, and in all things charity."

The *Q* represents *questions*. CRI answers people's questions regarding cults, culture, and Christianity.

The *U* represents *user friendly*. CRI is committed to taking complex issues and making them understandable and accessible to the lay Christian.

The *I* stands for *integrity*. Recall Paul's admonition: "Watch your life and doctrine closely. Persevere in them, because if you do, you will save both yourself and your hearers" (1 Tim 4:16).

Finally, the *P* represents *parachurch*. CRI is committed to the local church as the God-ordained vehicle for equipping, evangelism, and education.

Contact Christian Research Institute:

By Mail:
CRI International
P.O. Box 8500
Charlotte, NC 28271-8500

FAX
(704) 887-8299

By Phone:
24-hour Customer Service (U.S.):
(704) 887-8200
24-hour Toll-Free Credit Card Line:
(888) 7000-CRI

On the Internet:
www.equip.org

In Canada:
CRI Canada
56051 Airways P.O
Calgary, Alberta T2E 8K5

For information (Canada:)
(403) 571-6363
24-hour Customer Service
(800) 665-5851

On the Broadcast:
To contact the *Bible Answer Man* broadcast with your questions, call toll free in the U.S. and Canada, 1(888) ASK HANK (275-4265), Monday-Friday, 5:30 p.m. to 7:00 p.m. Eastern Time.

For a list of stations airing the *Bible Answer Man* or to listen to the broadcast via the Internet, log on to www.equip.org.

Other Fine Books on This Subject from Tyndale House Publishers

NON-FICTION

The DaVinci Deception,
by Irwin Lutzer.
Softcover.
ISBN-13: 978-1-4143-0633-9
ISBN-10: 1-4143-0633-4

Jesus, Lover of a Woman's Soul,
by Irwin and Rebecca Lutzer.
Hardcover.
ISBN-13: 978-0-8423-8426-1
ISBN-10: 0-8423-8426-X

FICTION

Magdalene, by Angela Hunt.
Softcover.
ISBN-13: 978-1-4143-1028-2
ISBN-10: 1-4143-1028-5

Maggie's Story,
by Dandi Daley Mackall.
Softcover.
ISBN-13: 978-1-4143-0978-1
ISBN-10: 1-4143-0978-3

Divine, by Karen Kingsbury.
Hardcover.
ISBN-13: 978-1-4143-0765-7
ISBN-10: 1-4143-0765-9